Ronnie Barker

Ronnie Barker
The Authorised Biography

CHAMELEON

Bob McCabe

First published in Great Britain in 1998 by Chameleon Books

an imprint of André Deutsch Ltd

76 Dean Street

London W1V 5HA

André Deutsch Ltd is a VCI plc company

www.vci.co.uk

Design: Neal Townsend for JMP Ltd

Picture research: Karen Tucker for JMP Ltd

Printed in England by Butler & Tanner Ltd, Frome and London

Origination by Digicol England

A catalogue record for this book is available from the British Library

ISBN 0 233 99382 7

Contents

ACKNOWLEDGEMENTS, OR THE BIT MOST PEOPLE DON'T READ

I can't remember a single point in my life when I didn't know who Ronnie Barker was. He has been a firm fixture in my consciousness since, well, forever. *The Two Ronnies*, Arkwright, *Porridge*: I, like countless others, grew up watching his every move. And, it goes without saying, laughing. Hard. When the chance came to write a book on Ronnie Barker, my first thought was *Porridge*. You see, when I watch *Porridge*, then or now, I don't see the man from *The Two Ronnies*. I can see how Arkwright might be related to him. But not Fletcher. Having now met the man and spent numerous hours talking and eating with him, I look at *Porridge* now... And I still don't see that man I had several rather fine chilis with. That to me is the test of a truly great actor.

This book bears the word 'biography' in its title, but to be honest this isn't a biography in the strictest sense. It is a biography not of a life, but of a career. Ronnie is a very private man and didn't really want the ins and outs of his private areas exposed (as it were). And quite rightly so; what counts here is a superb body of work. His life is his own. But his work belongs to all of us.

It would be quite facile for me to thank him for all the countless hours of laughter he has given me via the box in the corner of the living room, but I've never had a problem with being facile. And, having re-watched many of those hours in the course of writing this book, I remain thankful.

More importantly, I'd like to thank him for the time and help he gave me during the writing of this book. For a man who hasn't really given an interview in the last decade, he was remarkably forthcoming, informative and, of course, entertaining. A good deal of the book is him verbatim – I figured I had the horse's mouth; that's the best part of the animal to have. Equally forthcoming with their time were a number of people who have played key roles in Ronnie's career. I am indebted to Ronnie Corbett for being so charming and generous in talking about his old partner. Josephine Tewson, June Whitfield and Sydney Lotterby were also a great help, generous with their time and very genuine in their warm regard for the subject at hand. I would also like to thank Sir Peter Hall for taking time out of a hectic rehearsal period to fill me in on Ronnie's early days in London. (He may well regret it if people decide to blame him for Ronnie's retirement – really, it wasn't his fault!)

David Jason remains one of the most important relationships in Ronnie's life, professionally and personally, and his insights were a great help to this book, which would, I'm sure, be a lot poorer without them. And so to the people you won't have heard of... for their support, creativity and, let's be honest, the cash, I'd like to thank Mal Peachey and John Conway of JMP, fine publishers that they are. For their enduring friendship, loyalty, offers of employment and, let's be honest, the cash, a special thank you to Rob Churchill, Mark Kermode, Alan Jones, Nigel Floyd and Simon Rose. For sneaking some tapes out of the BBC on my behalf, a big cheers to Michael Samuels.

Additional thanks to Joan and Trevor Churchill for the use of their tape!

I am also indebted to the staff of the Crown and Cushion Hotel (when in Chipping Norton, use no other!) and the Selsdon Park Hotel in Croydon.

I also owe a great deal to the staff at the BBC News Information Service who, trust me, helped me much more than they know.

Much love and thanks as always to Mary McCabe, in this instance for her infinite knowledge of quiz shows and their relationship to the works of Dickens (you'll have to read the book to work that one out).

Finally, for love, understanding and more love, I am eternally indebted to one Lucy Merritt and a certain Jessie McCabe, whose half-hourly interruptions in the form of a clenched fist banging on a locked study door while shouting 'DADDY!' over and over again were a constant source of delight.

(Oh yeah, and I'd like to thank the makers of Gameboy for their wonderful products, which provided literally hours of distraction during the making of this book – yes, Mal and John, that's why it was late!)

BOB McCABE *February 1998*

Foreword
by David Jason

To any keen watcher of television over the last thirty years or so, the name Ronnie Barker has always meant a guarantee of entertainment in its highest possible form. His name has meant that a programme in which he is to appear will ensure an evening to remember for perhaps the entire nation. He has shared his natural and perfect gift of comedy with us all. There is no one in showbusiness who can come anywhere near his multiplicity of talent and I doubt that anyone ever will.

I have been fortunate indeed to have shared so many happy and funny hours with Ronnie, not only on a working basis, but also at his home with he and his lovely wife, Joy (who also has a wonderful sense of humour and a very sharp wit) and the rest of the warm and friendly Barker family.

On the following pages of this book one will learn a little more about this very clever man's early career and rise to fame. Anything which gives us an insight into his great talent is worth a read.

It is impossible to sum up in a few words the full extent of Ronnie's comic gift, but to give just a hint of the R.B. I've known and loved, I can relate the following tale: One day during rehearsals for *Open All Hours*, he and I invented some very silly and funny piece of business which made both of us laugh long and loud. As we began to subside, Ronnie turned to me and remarked, quite seriously, 'Aren't we lucky. Here we are both getting paid just to make ourselves laugh!' I would like to add, 'Yes, but you've also made the nation laugh, too'.

David Jason O.B.E.

Ronnie with David Jason and his British Comedy Lifetime Achievement Award, 1990.

Chapter ONE

To Begin At The End

'**YOU** and I will never get on, Ron. You have to be queer to get on.' The time is late 1954. The location a pub in Oxford, a place popular with the actors and stage crew of the nearby Oxford Playhouse. The speaker would go on to cast a mighty shadow over 20th century British theatre. The speakee would go on to become British television's best-loved comedy actor. When rising theatre director Peter Hall, a couple of pints down, told struggling young actor Ronnie Barker that their chances in the theatre were next to nothing, he was, in retrospect, most assuredly wrong.

Peter Hall was not only to have a profound effect on British theatre, but on Ronnie Barker's career. He was the man who took Ronnie to the West End in 1955. Around thirty years later, he was the man who was responsible for Barker

offer. "Let me know when you'll be available." Which was another wonderful thing, because in other words it meant, "Whenever you're ready, we'll do it." So I asked, "How long will it be?" And he replied, "We'll rehearse eight to ten weeks for the two plays, you'll only play about four times a week because we'll be in repertory..." So I asked to think it over. I lived in Pinner then, and I said to myself, "Now, what time should I leave to deal with the traffic?" Then I suddenly did a mental double take and said to myself, "Wait a minute. If your first priority when you've been offered this wonderful part at the National Theatre is how you're going to get through the traffic, you really shouldn't be in this business anymore. Your priorities have drifted right away from the business, they are about how to stay comfortable and not get stressed in traffic."

'So I wrote to PETER HALL and I said,
"Thank you for your offer, I've considered it
and I'M GOING TO RETIRE"'

retiring at the height of his fame and popularity.

'I don't think I've said this anywhere, but Peter Hall was the man who caused me to retire,' says Barker, 'because he wrote to me a couple of years before I retired, about 1986, and said, "Would you come to the National to do *Henry IV 1 & 2*, to play Falstaff?" Which was a wonderful

So I wrote to Peter and I said, "Thank you for your offer, I've considered it and I'm going to retire." I didn't retire the next week, I planned it and it happened 18 months later. But that really was the time when I thought, "Look, you've had enough. You really have no more ambition left." '

Early Days

Ronald William George Barker – sounds like a banker's name, doesn't it? Which is appropriate, really, given that one of Ronald Barker's first stabs at employment was in a bank. A fortuitous move, really, for it was here that young Ronald met a colleague who persuaded him to have a go at local amateur dramatics 'just for something to do socially'. Acting, so often referred to by those in the profession as a bug, did indeed bite, although this was by no means his first experience of the theatre.

Ronald William George Barker was born on 25 September, 1929, in the town of Bedford, the middle child of three, to mother Edith and father Leonard. When he was four, his father's job as an oil clerk for Shell saw the family relocate to Oxford, where Ronald spent his childhood. Although his father was named Leonard, everyone called him Tim. The reason why is

something that seems lost to the mists of time, it just was. 'Leonard William Barker. Known as Tim.' It was Tim Barker who used to take his family to the theatre.

'We would stand in the long queue,' recalls Ronnie. 'There was a queue for ninepence and a queue for one and threepence and if they ran out of ninepence tickets we went home. That's how much money we could afford. It's funny how many comedians, actor-comedians, come from working class backgrounds. It's amazing. I don't know what generates it in a working class environment but it seems as though they have to have something to laugh at. It must be a way out.'

The first play they saw was called *Cottage To Let*, starring Alastair Sim and a young George Cole, then an evacuee protégé of Sim's. Years later, Sim would return the compliment, coming to see Ronald Barker in a production of *Listen To*

MARGARET *was one of the few actors* *Ronald ever* **OFFERED ADVICE** *to. 'If I were you,' he told her, 'I'd* **GIVE UP'** *(Maggie Smith now has two Oscars to her name)*

The Wind at the Oxford Playhouse, even taking the time to drop by backstage, much to the young actor's surprise.

The Barkers also used to go to the panto. 'Pantos were wonderful, they really were. We were in the gods. I was a bit frightened to actually walk along the front row because it was such a steep drop.'

Ronnie Barker told his first joke in public at the a very young age. 'There was then a gap of about ten years before I made my next joke.' The first happened by chance during a poetry recital.

'It was in my junior school. We were standing up and reciting the poems we were supposed to have learned or read. This is way back. A boy called Thornton – I still remember his name – stood up and his poem was something about a windmill. He said, "The windmill cuts through the air, cuts through the air, cuts through the air." And I said, "He'll be bald in a minute with all

that 'air cutting." I remember saying that and I was eight. It went down well, except with the master. He didn't actually do anything but he reprimanded me.'

This incident aside it was, for the most part, a quiet childhood for Ronald Barker, the exceptions being his singing in the St James Church Choir, and his contracting, at the age of eight, a kidney infection which led to four months in hospital. He was served rice pudding every day for the whole four months and claims to this day to have never eaten it since.

He attended the City of Oxford High School, finding the name of former pupil T E Lawrence (later Lawrence of Arabia) in one of his text books. 'I must have been vaguely amusing when I was a teenager, I guess, but I was never known as the life and soul of the party.' It was wartime, and trips to the theatre or the movies were rare, with radio often taking their place. 'I was twelve

(Right) Ronnie as Norman Stanley Fletcher in an early publicity still for Porridge, 1974.

or thirteen. I think that's when I started to appreciate funny-line comedy. Radio was the thing and you never missed a minute of it. I was a big admirer of Tommy Handley and *ITMA* (*It's That Man Again*), as it was called. I started to enjoy radio comedy then.'

On leaving school he studied as an architect. Among his class mates were Ian and Alistair Smith. 'I went for six months then I gave it up because I realised I wasn't good enough,

fire. 'The first time I went and we sat in the stalls and the curtain went up, it was the first rep I'd seen and I thought it was wonderful.' So much so, in fact, that the young bank clerk was soon writing to the company asking for work. At first he sent them a photo. When he heard nothing from them he wrote again, asking for the photo back. This got him an audition.

He auditioned for the company's director Horace Wentworth by reading in six different

'It was the FOURTH WEEK of my PROFESSIONAL career and I thought that's it, I WANT TO BE FUNNY'

because they were so good and they were in the same form. So I thought, it's an overcrowded profession so I should walk out now. And I did. I walked out, left all my equipment there, my brushes and pens and drawing boards. And I think it was the best thing I ever did in my life.'

Barker would meet up with Alistair and Ian Smith a few years later, when their sister Margaret joined the company at the Oxford Playhouse. Margaret was one of the few actors Ronald ever offered advice to. 'If I were you,' he told her, 'I'd give up.' Maggie Smith now has two Oscars to her name.

Realising that architecture was not for him, Barker inherited his older sister Vera's job in the local bank. The work was dull but at least it led to his debut on the stage, albeit in The Theatre Players' local amateur productions. A trip to see the Manchester Repertory Company, playing in Aylesbury, soon added fuel to Barker's theatrical

accents, a natural talent that had grown out of his penchant for radio comedy. Wentworth hired him on the spot, something that caused Barker some consternation as he had to work out a week's notice at the bank. Wentworth gave him the week and the following Monday Ronald Barker began his life as a theatre professional.

A Reputable Life

Barker started as an assistant stage manager, the theatrical term for general dogsbody, largely involved in props but almost instantly finding his way onto the stage in a small role in a production of *Quality Street*. Having spent up to four months at a time rehearsing amateur shows, life in rep came as something of a shock. 'It was different mainly because of the work rate, which was amazing. I think most young actors today would say, "I can't do that, I need three weeks rehearsal." You had one week of

rehearsal but you'd opened the night before in another play. Then, on the Tuesday, following the Monday first night, you started the next play. So you were playing a play and rehearsing a play at the same time and I was also on props so I was also thinking of the play after that. I could only learn my lines in bed at night. We only rehearsed in the mornings but I was busy with the props in the afternoon. Rehearsal time was ridiculous. You did about ten hours in all for the whole play and then on you went. That was the main difference. Suddenly, you had to throw yourself on to a moving vehicle. But it was wonderful training. People said at the time that

was doing the music – we were using 78rpm records – and I had to put on the music, do curtain call, take out the music and run down the stairs on to the stage, the curtain was up and I there I was, on stage eating flies. It was a terrible four seconds.'

By his second production, *When We Are Married*, Barker felt completely at home on the stage, having been rapidly assimilated into the group by the hectic work rate. It was in his fourth week, however, that Barker was to discover the thing that would become his life's work – comedy. 'It was the fourth week of my professional career and I thought, "That's it, I

'He completely **INHABITED** what it was he was **PLAYING**, even if it was a north country **CHARWOMAN**'

SIR PETER HALL

rep was a bit dangerous because you got into habits, because of the speed of things. I think that was a good thing for me because when we did *Two Ronnies* we only rehearsed for a week. Mind you, it wasn't a two and a half hour play, but it had to be more concentrated and more precise because of television. I think it was a good training to have to get it into your head. It was certainly good for learning.'

One of Barker's many roles at Aylesbury was that of the fly-chomping Renfield in *Dracula,* a production that neatly demonstrates the rigours of life in rep. 'We did *Dracula* and I was ASM at the same time. I was playing Renfield, the maniac who eats flies. And he opens the play. I

want to be funny." I was playing the chauffeur in *Miranda*, and the character had some funny lines. That was the first funny part I played. I played a funny part of sorts in *When We Are Married*, which was the second thing I did. I played Gerald, the juvenile, in that. He has some lines but the fun was in the situation. But it was actually the chauffeur in *Miranda* that got a laugh on a funny line. I heard this big laugh and thought, "God, that's marvellous. It's wonderful." I suddenly thought that's what I wanted to do. Whether I said that to myself, consciously or not, that's what I felt. From then on I looked for the comedy parts. You got what you were given in rep, of course, especially in that sort of rep, because there were only certain people who could do certain things. But by December 1948 I'd already decided that I wanted to play the funny parts.'

It wasn't just the thrill of the laugh, the joy of judging and delivering the timing. Barker soon discovered an innate ability for comedy, something within him that just understood 'funny'. 'I think I did. I don't want to sound in any way big-headed, but I never had to think about timing a laugh. I never came off a stage and thought, "I mis-timed that line." I never had to do that because I said it how I say it. That's why it's always been difficult for me to take direction. Also to rewrite comedy. Because people say, "I think that could be better written." I say, "Well, I can't write it any better because I've written it already and I've written it in the best way I think it can be." I was always like that in acting. If a director points out something, say you've hit the wrong inflection, I can take that. But if somebody says, "You shouldn't be feeling what you're feeling there." I would say, "Well, I can't change that." So I was a difficult person to direct in a way.'

Ronald's first starring role at Aylesbury was also to be his last. He took the lead in their production of *The Guinea Pig* by W Chetham Strode, a controversial play in its day, which required the young actor to say 'arse' on stage. His mother wasn't too happy, but Barker was when he learned that Armitage Owen, the overall boss of their rep company, was transferring the production to the Pavilion Theatre in Rhyl, north Wales, and he was going with it. Sadly, during his time in Rhyl the Aylesbury rep company was disbanded. Those left in Rhyl didn't last much longer and soon the Manchester Repertory Company was no more, and Ronald Barker was an unemployed actor.

Barker's next professional stint was as a mime with the Mime Theatre Company. It would be fair to call it the low point of his career, dogged by a heavy dose of flu and, eventually, a long walk back to Oxford from Penzance when the now-bust company's coffers would only stretch to five train tickets and Ronald proved to be unlucky number six.

A quick trawl through *The Stage* soon secured some stage management work at Frank H Fortescue's Famous Players, a rep company based in Bramhall, Cheshire. It was here that Barker was to meet one of the most influential men in his career. Glenn Melvyn was the company's leading man and the man who Barker claims 'was to teach me everything I ever learned about comedy'.

Within a few years, Melvyn would be starring in the West End in *The Love Match*, a play he wrote for Arthur Askey, and would have his own television series, called *I'm Not Bothered*. Barker would get his first television acting and writing experience on that show and would later repay the debt to Melvyn by casting him in *The Fastest Gun In Finchley* episode of *The Ronnie Barker Playhouse*.

Oxford still held an allure for the young actor. It was his home town, and Ronald had long admired the company at the Oxford Playhouse. Among the many performers he had seen at the theatre was a young Tony Hancock. 'I saw Hancock in the pantomime, with Frank Shelley, who was one of the three men who furthered my career. Hancock was a very thin ugly sister and very funny. John Moffat, who was a favourite there, was also in it. Tony Hancock just showed up. I don't know how he got there. He was obviously just an actor who suddenly branched out into comedy, rather like I did, I suppose. You never hear it referred to. I was reading something about Hancock's life, but it never mentioned that. Because I was such a fan of John Moffat, Tony Hancock didn't stick out as much as if I'd gone with an open mind. Moffat was the epitome of wit and clever characterisation which, naturally, I liked. So my eyes were on him most of the time.' So, when Barker learned that two of his old friends from amateur days were working backstage at the Playhouse, he wrote to Frank Shelley and was invited for an interview. The job he was offered was in publicity, but Oxford was his Mecca and any means of getting in there was enough for him to say goodbye to Bramhall and return home.

Having quickly found his way out of distributing handbills and on to the Playhouse stage, Barker spent three years at Oxford. It was here that he gave the bad advice to Maggie Smith and received some from Peter Hall, then a bright young hope of British theatre, paying his pre-West End dues. 'What I remember about him right from the beginning at Oxford,' says the now-knighted Peter Hall, 'was that he was an extraordinarily gifted actor. The thing that struck me was that he had the gift of total relaxation. It's what all actors strive for. And allied to that he had immaculate comic timing. Absolutely immaculate. And I think that in all his comedy, all his acting, right from the very beginning, you had an awareness of the performer, a rather genial but rather cryptic personality, commenting on what he's saying. I just thought he was going to have a spectacular acting career. If you'd said to me then he was going to become a great comic, and a comic writer, I probably wouldn't have known what you were talking about. I always regarded him as a great actor. And still do. The measure of his comedy

was that he was absolutely true. He completely inhabited what it was he was being, even if it was a north country charlady.'

Two men and two events prompted Barker to move from Oxford. The first was Glenn Melvyn, who had by now written a sequel to *The Love Match* and asked Barker to join the touring cast of the play. As Arthur Askey was no longer involved, Melvyn had moved into the lead role, leaving the key second billed role open for Ronald. It was for this part that Melvyn taught him the comedy stutter he later used to such effect in *Open All Hours*, an acknowledgement that Barker has always been keen to stress. The second element was Peter Hall. Hall had been asked to direct a production of Eugene O'Neill's *Mourning Becomes Electra* at the Arts Theatre in London. A small theatre, yes, but still, it was London. He asked Barker to join him.

Two-Timing In London

From January to May 1955, Ronald Barker toured with Glenn Melvyn. In June he started rehearsing for his London debut.

'It was where everybody wanted to be. It was a milestone. I was glad, because at the Playhouse the rut was setting in. I'd been living at home for four years, so he took me away from that.'

Life in London moved too fast for any possible rut to become well-worn. Following *Mourning Becomes Electra*, Peter Hall moved Ronald into the West End for his next production, *Summertime*, at the Apollo Theatre. Dirk Bogarde and Geraldine McEwan were the leads. Around Christmas time, Hall started work on a production of Vivian Ellis's *Listen To The Wind*, a play they had recently staged at Oxford and one that was to create a unique opportunity for the young actor just beginning to make his

Playing the Head Waiter opposite Frankie Vaughan in his first film, Wonderful Things!, *1958.*

'I'm of the **OPINION** that a lot of characters that people play are quite **SHALLOW**. I don't mean the person is shallow or the actor is shallow, but you **LAY IT ON** to yourself like a thin layer of **ICING**'

name in the London theatre world. 'At Oxford, I had a part in the first act and a small part in the second act. But a good part in the first, a sort of mad gypsy song and dance. Peter said, "It's a pity you can't play the gypsy man again." And I suddenly thought, "Well, why can't I?" He said, "What do you mean, you're in *Summertime*?" And I said, "But I'm only in the third act there... I could do the first act of this one at the Arts, then I've got all of the second act to nip round and get ready for the next one. I can do a composite make up – one's a yokel and one's a gypsy." He said, "It hasn't been done for years." It was last done in 1935 or something. So he told me to go home and work out the times. The times were different, especially Saturday matinees, so I went home and worked out a time sheet. It was a bit of a rush on Saturdays. It was only four minutes away through Gerrard Street and onto Shaftesbury Avenue.'

'He's a phenomenal hard worker,' says Peter Hall. 'And we simply couldn't not have him in *Listen To The Wind*, he'd been so marvellous in it at Oxford.'

Playing two different roles in two different plays, with a four-minute dash in between, proved in no way a strain for the young actor. In many ways, it was this that led him to explore his approach to characterisation, something that would become a trademark of his career. 'I've never had that problem of separating characters. I can do *Porridge* now, immediately followed by Arkwright, immediately followed by anyone you care to mention. Because, you see, I'm of the opinion that a lot of characters that people play are quite shallow. I don't mean the person is shallow or the actor is shallow, but you lay it on to yourself like a thin layer of icing. So it's easy to just shift along. I had no problem at all, so I did it. I did twenty-two shows a week and I got £27 for the week. I was getting £15 a week for *Summertime* and £12 for the gypsy man at the Arts. Ridiculous, but that was a wonderful moment.'

This unintentional piece of theatrical grandstanding paid off in spades. Having played two roles at once, Barker was now being offered several others, moving first into a production of *Double Image* at the Savoy Theatre with Richard Attenborough.

A short break from the West End in late 1956 proved equally fortuitous, when Barker met young actress/ASM Joy Tubb in a Cambridge production of Somerset Maugham's *The Letter*. They married the following July. 'Joy Tubb she was then. She was glad to get rid of her name, she's always said that. We went to a BBC party recently and they had all the names and they had her down as Joy Tubb again. She said, "I got rid of that name 40 years ago." ' Among the many things they had in common was their love of Laurence Olivier. As a star-struck teenager, Joy had stood outside Olivier's house for hours on end in hope of catching a glimpse of him; as an actor Barker later said he always approached his characters by starting with the make-up. 'If it's good enough for Olivier, it's good enough for me. He used to do it that way.

'Olivier was always my idol. In fact, one of my sons is called Laurence. My wife was a great fan so when we met and both realised we were mad about Olivier, naturally our first son was named Laurence.'

Barker was quickly back in the West End, courtesy of Peter Hall again, this time in *Camino Real* at the Phoenix. But by now theatre was not the only medium being exposed to Barker's burgeoning talents

Larking About On Radio

Radio comedy was something that young Ronald Barker had grown up on, shows like *ITMA*, *Up The Pole* and *Stand Easy* were all early favourites. Indeed, listening to the radio nurtured his talent for characters, voices and accents as well his fondness for line comedy. His first radio appearance was as a regular supporting player on *The Floggits* in 1956. The show starred Elsie and Doris Waters, and featured Anthony Newley, Joan Sims and the newly christened 'Ronnie' Barker. 'The director Alastair Scott-Johnson did that. Without telling me. The first *Radio Times* I was in, it was Ronnie. I thought, "Ronnie. Is that all right?" He said he thought it sounded more friendly, more

chummy. I'm glad he did. I was still Ronald in a lot of the plays. Ronald's a bit pompous really. It's a funny name.'

Ronnie's stint on *The Floggits* was to prove short-lived, however. The reason? He was too funny. 'Tony Newley and I got sacked from that because we were getting too many laughs. It's funny, because I always thought Hancock did the same thing, he got rid of all the comedians round him. We said this to Elsie and Doris, or at least the producer said it. "This is your show, girls. These fellas will get laughs from you, of course they will, but that makes a funny show. You must have a funny show." So they said, "Why can't we have funny lines?" "Well, you do have funny lines but you can't have these characters' lines, you can't have the catchphrases that these men come on and say – God knows why, but catchphrases do make people laugh – "And it's goodnight from him." Extraordinary. But they got rid of us.'

Getting the sack has never seemed to be a problem for Ronnie Barker. It would happen again in 1970. The result of that would be a move to the BBC and the creation of *The Two Ronnies*. This time round, however, it found him back in the West End, at the Royal Court in a production of *Lysistrata*. 'Lysistrata was an extraordinary performance, really, because it was directed by a Greek director called Minos Volanarkis who liked certain scenes and didn't like others. He'd only rehearse scenes he liked, which was a bit upsetting for we who considered ourselves not old pros but professionals. Jimmy Grout was in it, Joan Greenwood, Natasha Parry, various people. And Minos wouldn't join the scenes. There were fourteen scenes and he wouldn't join one to the other. So you'd finished the scene and I'd be over this side of the stage and Neil

McCarthy or someone would be over there and we'd go to the next scene and we'd all be in different places. I said, "Minos, are you ever going to put these together?" and he'd say, "Oh, yes." But, of course, when it came to the dress rehearsal it still wasn't done. So I said to Jimmy Grout, "What are we going to do?" And he said, "We'd better do it ourselves." So I asked the

Bull. Having accidentally ruined one of the old postcards on Bull's mirror, Ronnie went to a nearby stall selling similar cards at a penny a time. He bought a hundred, meaning to give them to Bull, but became so entranced by these pieces of Edwardiana that he kept fifty of them for himself. His collection now stands at 55,000.

'I'm a very nostalgic person. I collect many

> **'I was TERRIFIED because I'd heard that if you moved an inch on TELEVISION, if you MOVED ONE INCH to the right or left, you were out of shot. Which was RUBBISH, of course'**

others if it would be alright if Jimmy and I work out the links and they said, "Please do." And Minos never even noticed when he had a run-through. And we'd done it all.

'Jimmy was very funny, because it was considered an immoral and maybe disgusting play, about women denying their men any sexual whatevers if they carried on fighting because they wanted to stop the war. There were a lot of phallic jokes in it. And one night from the gallery came floating down a sort of snowstorm of leaflets saying, "This play is disgusting." Jimmy Grout was on stage. He looked up and saw this snowstorm and suddenly said, "The Gods are angry!" I wish I'd said that.'

It was during the run of *Lysistrata* that Ronnie was to discover one of the other passions of his life. He was sharing a dressing room with Peter

things that have nostalgia value. I collect cigarette cards, for instance, and I certainly collect the old postcards. I collect old coins and stamps because I used to collect stamps as a boy and loved it. And paper work. I have theatre programmes, illustrated sheet music. I have lantern slides. I have stereoscopic photo viewers, everything that can be loosely termed paper ephemera. I just love that sort of stuff. And I love illustrations. I've got copies of the summer and Christmas issues of *Tatler* and *Punch* which were wonderfully illustrated in colour. I also collect illustrated books.'

Having successfully played in *The Love Match* and its sequel, Glenn Melvyn was now a hot property in the burgeoning new medium of television. He was offered his own show, *I'm Not Bothered*, and he asked his old friend and colleague Ronnie Barker to join him in several episodes. *I'm Not Bothered* was to prove a vital stepping stone in Ronnie's career. Not only did it offer him the first chance to work before a camera in a medium he would come to dominate, it also allowed him to try his hand at writing comedy material for the first time, something he would continue to do – under a series of pseudonyms – for the rest of his career. 'Glenn got this television series and asked if would I like to play a part. He also asked if I would like to do some ghost-writing, which was I suppose the first time I wrote anything. I got £50 a script for that, which was a bit of a joke, but it was good for me then because I had no money. So he said would I like to be in it and I said yes. I was terrified, 'cause I'd heard that if you moved an inch on television, if you moved one inch to the right or left, you were out of shot. Which was rubbish, of course. I don't know who told me that. I was terrified about this but when I got there I found I was playing a patient in bed and I didn't have to move. So I was very relieved.'

Ronnie wrote three scripts for the show, all of which were attributed to Melvyn himself. 'I remember the director Henry Kendal, in his later years – he wasn't working as much as he had been in his heyday – directed one of the shows I was in and he didn't know I'd written it, 'cause Glenn didn't tell anyone. He just said, "Will you write it and I'll put my name to it? Is that alright?" He directed a couple of these and mine came up and in the bar afterwards I said, "That went very well, Mr Kendal, didn't it?" And he said, "Bit of quality in the writing, old boy." And I still couldn't tell him, but I was delighted with that. That was the first praise I'd had for my writing. Amazing.'

Writing was an interesting experience for Barker, but not an easy one. 'It's never been easy. I never enjoyed the actual physical act of writing. When it works it's wonderful, like in a *Two Ronnies* sketch, or the little silent films. When it works and you hear the audience laugh, you're very pleased and very proud of it. But actually getting it on to paper I find very painful. Because I very rarely re-write anything. I re-write it all in my head before I put it all down, if you see what I mean. Some people will put something down, then go back and fiddle with it until they get it right. I do it all in long hand, I don't use a typewriter, so I very rarely wrote anything before I sorted it out in my head. I found it was a painful process.'

Having experienced theatre, radio and television, it was only a matter of time before film came calling on Ronald. When it did, it came in the form of the long-forgotten 1958 *Wonderful Things!*, a vehicle for a young Frankie Vaughan, who starred as a Portuguese fisherman off to London to earn his fortune, no less. Ronnie played the role of the Head Waiter. 'I was cast by a man called Ronnie Curtis. We used to go into the Arts Theatre snack bar just below the Arts Theatre. It was a place where everyone met, all the out of work actors. And Ronnie Curtis was a cross-eyed talent scout/agent who had an office three doors away. He used to come into the Arts Theatre and look round and pick someone. He'd say "You!" – you never knew who he was picking. Michael Caine used to be there, Sean Connery used to be there, Ian Hendry and Roger Moore sometimes. All these young men were waiting for a day's work. But he came in and pointed at me and said, "I want to talk to you." He said, "I want you to be a head waiter in a new film." It was two day's work, over a week, which means you're available for a week and they can pick any two days. So off I went for my first

'Michael *CAINE* used to be there, Sean
CONNERY used to be there, Ian *HENDRY*
and Roger *MOORE* sometimes. All these
young men were *WAITING* for a day's work.
But he came in and pointed at *ME*...'

screen work, which was extraordinary.'

In radio, Ronnie was now working on *Variety Playhouse* with Ted Ray, June Whitfield and Leslie Crowther, who soon became a close and trusted friend. 'Leslie Crowther and I, or Ted Ray and I, did the low comedy, and the opera singers from Covent Garden would come. It was a wonderful mish-mash of a show, variety in its true sense, I suppose, a real mixture. But we loved it, especially Leslie. We used to arrive Sunday morning, sit in the stalls and listen to all the opera singers rehearse. And I remember Leslie was very tired, he'd been working very hard, and he was sat in the stalls and I remember looking round as this wonderful aria was being sung and tears were pouring down his face. He was a very emotional fellow and I miss him. I miss him. He was a great friend. But it was a great show and we used to say, "We're being paid for this as well?" Our work was far from onerous because you got a script, you see. All you had to do was stand there and read it. Wonderful. That's why radio's such a doddle really.'

It was all going too well, of course. 'Then I went into *Irma La Douce*, which drove me mad.' Ronnie landed the role of Roberto in the West End production of *Irma La Douce*, which featured an all-star cast including John Neville, Clive Revill, Keith Michell, Julian Orchard and Elizabeth Seal. It proved, much to Ronnie's distress, to be a huge hit. Normally for any actor, such a guaranteed gig would be a good thing but Barker found it soul-destroying to be tied into a run that, for him, lasted two years. He even got to the point where he was physically ill before going on stage some nights. 'It's very difficult to explain how awful it is, because it's not like saying people go to work every day for years. But you have to do everything exactly as you did it before. You can't change the lines slightly if

With Jimmy Edwards in Six More Faces Of Jim, *1962.*

Ronnie and Jimmy Edwards as The Glums,
Six More Faces Of Jim, *1962.*

you're bored with them. You can in a stand-up act. Ronnie Corbett does his act, he puts bits in, takes bits out, does what he likes. But with this, you must not waver at all, a): because you've got all the other people round you and b): you're not in a position to be able to judge what is better or worse. That's the author or the director's job. It was the fact you had to sit down in the same place, do the same thing, say the same line, sing the same number... it was fine for the first six or nine months, I suppose. Everyone gets bored. I'd been told by the producer Donald Albery. "We can't give you a year's contract on paper. But believe me, if you want to leave after a year and you've got something to go to, I will let you go." And just over a year later, a musical version of *Sweeney Todd* came along and they wanted me to play Todd. I went to Albery's manager and said, "Mr Albery had said this" and she said, "No, he wouldn't have said that. He wouldn't have." I said, "But he did. He told me. Gentleman's agreement." And she said, "I'm sorry, but it's not on paper." I was furious.'

Six months later, however, Barker found a way out. The play was transferring to Broadway and Clive Revill, who played the narrator of the piece, was going with it. Ronnie had been understudying his role and was expected to take over. It was a bigger role and naturally meant more money. But Ronnie opted not to.

'I thought, "Well, why should I do that?" I explained. "It's a much harder part, much more energetic, he does a lot more changes. I'm comfortable where I am, thank you," knowing very well that this would rock the boat a bit. So about a fortnight later they said we're supposed to be going in ten days and we've got no one to play it. So I said. "Well, tell Mr Albery that I will play it for six weeks while you find someone

else, provided he lets me out of the show altogether." Blackmail it was, really. And he said, "Fine, but you won't work for me again." I said, "I'll have to risk that." And I was out, but it was such a relief and I never signed anything again like that.'

Life during *Irma La Douce* wasn't all bad, however. Barker's radio work continued, and in 1959 he landed himself the role of Able Seaman Johnson in one of the BBC's finest-ever radio half hours, *The Navy Lark*.

In 1958, writer Laurie Wyman had decided to build a series around rising comic actor Jon Pertwee, who had recently scored a success with his own radio show, *Pertwee's Progress*. Pertwee had himself served in the navy and it was quickly decided to build the show around the Senior Service. The rest of the cast were assembled, including Dennis Price, Michael Bates and Leslie Phillips. As Wyman told *Radio Times*, 'I felt we needed an idiot and there was no one better at playing idiots than Leslie Phillips.'

Ronnie Barker signed on for duty as one of the supporting players but was soon sharing the limelight with Pertwee, their interactions often proving the comic highlights of the shows. 'He was wonderful. I loved Jon. I thought he was a very good actor, I don't think he acted enough. Of course, he got into *Dr Who*, which was wonderful for him, but he got stuck with it a bit, I thought. But I thoroughly enjoyed working with him on stage.'

The series was set aboard the HMS Troutbridge, stationed in Portsmouth, and within three weeks of its first broadcast on 27 March 1959, the show was such a success that the film rights were sold. (In the somewhat uninspired movie version that followed, only the services of Leslie Phillips were retained.) By the second series, Price had left and was replaced by Stephen Murray, who remained on board for the show's following – and at the time record-breaking – seventeen-and-a-half year run.

By the second series, Seaman Johnson's role was expanding, becoming a favourite with the audience and, consequently, the scriptwriters. His oft repeated 'You're rotten, you are,' was all-but a catchphrase. In the show's fifth series, it briefly became *The TV Lark* with the crew commandeering a TV station – Troutbridge Commercial Television. The idea ran its course and after ten weeks they were back to the boat.

Overall, *The Navy Lark* was a huge success and Ronnie remained with the show for nine years, up until his appearances on *The Frost Report* made him unavailable for the show's recordings.

Facing Up To Jimmy Edwards

By the early 1960s, Ronnie Barker was juggling radio work on *The Navy Lark* and the occasional guest spot on Michael Bentine's *Round The Bend* with another West End role, this time in a production of *Platanov*. He was by no means a famous face but his voice was instantly recognisable thanks to *The Navy Lark*. More importantly, he was beginning to be known within the industry as a reliable, talented and extremely funny performer.

He had appeared on television again in a live schools broadcast of extracts from *Macbeth*, and was briefly seen on the popular early evening *Tonight* programme, a current affairs show. Ronnie and Prunella Scales appeared as a human cartoon strip. 'We were dressed in cardboard all the time. I had a cardboard moustache and a cardboard hat and she had a cardboard boater on. She was a schoolgirl and it

had little jokes like a cartoon strip would have.'

Television was in its infancy at this time, but it was still something of a golden age, especially in terms of its writers. Hancock had successfully transferred his *Half Hour* to the medium, courtesy of the work of Ray Galton and Alan Simpson. Another team of writers, Frank Muir and Dennis Norden, were also coming into their own, writing a series for the blustery, moustached comedy actor Jimmy Edwards, already a huge star on radio courtesy of *Take It From Here*, which featured a young June Whitfield.

The Playhouse format was dominant – in which the name performer would star in a series of half-hour shows, playing a different character in a different situation each week. *The Seven Faces Of Jim* was Muir and Norden's first vehicle for Edwards and it proved a vital link in bringing Ronnie Barker fully into the medium in which he would one day quite literally set up shop.

James Gilbert was producing. He had also produced Stanley Baxter's television show *On The Bright Side*. When that show transferred to the stage, now called *On The Brighter Side*, and Baxter's on-screen feed, Richard Waring, was no longer available, Gilbert contacted Ronnie's agent. 'He said, "I'm looking for a sort of chubby chap to take over. Where can I see Ronnie working?" My agent said, "You can go to a radio show and watch him working from the audience so you can hear him and see him playing different characters." So one day they turned up. He'd brought Stanley Baxter with him and they watched it and they both decided I should do it.'

When a small part became available in *The Seven Faces Of Jim*, Gilbert looked no further than the man he had cast alongside Baxter.

'He said, "There's one line in one of the Jimmy Edwards pieces I'm going to do, would you like to come and do it?" It was only one line, as an announcer, but he said it was quite funny because this caption comes up underneath you saying "Judith Chalmers", who was a news reader at the time. So I said fine. And then the next week, he said, "There's two or three lines here you could do." Terence Alexander was in it and he was playing a villain called Sidney Figgins. The next day Terence rang through and said he was very ill. So Muir and Norden, who wrote it, said, "Well, we think Ronnie could do this part." '

He did it so well, in fact, that when the series was renewed for a second season – now titled *Six More Faces Of Jim* – Ronnie was made a co-star, alongside June Whitfield. The first episode even saw him cast as Ron Glum, the Glum family having been one of Edwards' biggest hits on the radio. 'My first impression of Ronnie was that he was rather talented,' recalled June Whitfield. 'He was always spot on with all his characters. He automatically picked something that was appropriate and amusing. We played all kinds of different roles. I think Ronnie enjoyed the variety of all that.'

'That was my first real television and after that people began to spot me. From that I started to get the other television work.' 1962's *Six More Faces Of Jim* became 1963's *More Faces Of Jim* and Ronnie Barker's own face was well on its way to becoming a well known one. ᴑᴑ

'He was always **SPOT-ON** with all his **CHARACTERS**. He automatically picked something that was appropriate and **AMUSING**'

JUNE WHITFIELD

Chapter TWO

Barker And The Bard... Briefly

FOR an actor who cites Laurence Olivier as an idol, Ronnie Barker has never really hankered after Shakespeare. Yet in 1962, sandwiched neatly between Jimmy Edwards' various *Faces Of...*, Shakespeare hankered after him, casting him in a Royal Court production of *A Midsummer Night's Dream*. It was a prestigious production, featuring talents such as Lynn Redgrave, Nicol Williamson, Rita Tushingham, Corin Redgrave and David Warner, another actor whom Ronnie had once offered advice to – 'You shouldn't be in this business. You're not cut out for it.' (Advising other actors was never Ronnie's strong suit.)

the Barker family's loaf, but movies still held an allure, offering as they did a touch of glamour. 'I suppose they were glamorous. I was pleased to be in them. Pleased to see them on the big screen. But they're even glamorous to me now. If I had been working and someone had offered me a big part, like Bob Hoskins has been offered, those sort of parts in American movies and things, I would have still found them glamorous.'

Throughout the early 1960s, Ronnie became one of what could almost be termed a floating repertory company in British cinema. The same faces showed up all the time, rarely leading, but always supporting ably. If it wasn't Bernard Cribbins it was Eric Sykes. If it wasn't Eric it was

> **'If I had been working and someone had offered me a BIG PART, like Bob HOSKINS has been offered, those sort of parts in AMERICAN movies and things, I would have still found them GLAMOROUS'**

This was Ronnie's first stab at the bard. Ironically, his only other attempt at all things iambic would be a decade later in a BBC television production of the very same play, this time cast as a heavily made-up Bottom.

By now, radio and television were buttering

Leslie Phillips. Or indeed Ronnie Barker. Made in 1962, *Kill Or Cure* was one such vehicle, featuring Barker, Sykes, Dennis Price, Terry-Thomas and Lionel Jeffries. 'I remember sitting talking to Lionel Jeffries. He was a grumbler, maybe, or gloomy. It was comic gloom, really.

'I suddenly started doing this **OLD CHAP** and it was **VERY SUCCESSFUL**. So that character sort of stayed at the back of my mind and he became Lord Rustless, because I **ENJOYED** playing him **SO MUCH**'

and he said. "Aren't things expensive these days?" I said, "Yes, they are." I said. "It cost me a hundred pounds a week just for house-keeping, just for running my house." "Two hundred and fifty it costs me," he said. Those are the little bits you remember, strange little things like that.'

Movies may have held an allure, television may have felt most natural, but the theatre kept the offers of work coming in. Ronnie starred as Bob Acres in *All In Love*, a musical version of Sheridan's *The Rivals*, before taking on the role of Lord Slingsby-Craddock in *Mr Whatnot*, by a young British playwright by the name of Alan Ayckbourn. 'That was done at the Arts Theatre. It was about a piano tuner who never spoke. I don't know if he was dumb, he was a young man, Chaplinesque, really, because a lot of it was physical. And everything was done without props. It was a very strange piece, it was lovely. Very funny. Certain props, action props, were left out. We had a tennis match on the stage and there was no ball. It took a lot of rehearsing. I was the umpire and at one point I'd picked up a

newspaper and was reading it and Alan, who was directing, said it would be nice if the ball hit that paper. And I said, "Well, why doesn't it split it right down the middle?" It got a very good laugh. It was very strange and quite surreal. A bit *Alice In Wonderland* in places – we were having a picnic in the garden and suddenly war broke out. We were attacked by the enemy and we were lobbing buns over the hedge. No props, of course.'

Ask Barker if the role of Lord Slingsby-Craddock was a prototype for one of his most enduring creations, Lord Rustless, and he answers the question before it's finished. 'Yes he was. Absolutely. He was Lord Rustless mark one. Definitely. I did a character at Oxford Rep and it was a part that was supposed to be played by a woman. Frank Shelley, who was running Oxford Rep and was God there, said, "No, we won't play it as a woman, because we haven't any women. Ronnie, you can play it as an old man." So I suddenly started doing this old chap and it was very successful. It worked very well. So that character sort of stayed at the back of my

All bound up in television, as The Incredible Mr Tanner; Ronnie Barker Playhouse.

mind and he became Lord Rustless, because I enjoyed playing him so much.'

Lord Rustless first appeared by name in Ronnie's 1968 series *The Ronnie Barker Playhouse*, before being spun off into 1969's *Hark At Barker* and the 1972 sitcom *His Lordship Entertains*. Although the character he played in *Futtock's End* was called General Futtock, Ronnie freely admits that this too was in fact Rustless, as was the nameless figure in the *Two Ronnies* specials, *The Picnic* and *By The Sea*.

Little did Ayckbourn know he was creating a figure that his actor would truly make his own. Not that *Mr Whatnot* was the playwright's last dealings with his Lordship – he penned the links for *Hark At Barker* under the pseudonym of Peter Caulfield. Ronnie meanwhile cites the actor Fred Emney as the inspiration for his characterisation.

'He doesn't sound like him, but he has that same wonderful character, in that he'd sit back and let the world go by and nothing affected him. I love that sort of comedy and the way he did it; very, very laid back he was. I used to see him at the Oxford Theatre. I was at the Playhouse and we were allowed to go to the matinees at the New Theatre for free, so we were always there. We saw wonderful plays there and there was one called *Blue For A Boy*, which had Fred Emney and Richard Hearne in, and I remember in the middle of a song this woman was singing to him, he put his hand in his coat and took out a bag of chips in newspaper and started eating his chips all through this number. And he offered her a chip. He did strange things like that.'

Ronnie Barker

Before Porridge *there was* The Cracksman, *1963*.

These Two Ronnies Walk Into A Bar

1963 introduced Ronnie to two of the people with whom he would come to share his life. The first was a fictional character, the second was serving drinks standing – if you believe Barker's more prosaic recollections – on a crate so that he could actually see over the bar he was tending. The latter was Ronnie Corbett. The former was Norman Stanley Fletcher. At the time, of course, Ronnie failed to recognise the import of either meeting, particularly given that he met Fletch under another name.

Years later, while filming *Porridge,* Ronnie was surprised by an old publicity photo of himself in the Charlie Drake movie, *The Cracksman*. The look was the same, the prison uniform was the same, the hair was the same. Snout in his pocket, gum in his mouth – take away the scar on his face and this was Fletcher as a boy, doing porridge for the first time in the life of a 'habitual criminal who accepts arrest as an occupational hazard and presumably accepts imprisonment in the same casual manner'.

Looking back years later, Ronnie would realise that the seeds of his performance as Fletcher were sown in *The Cracksman*. 'We had a frightening time in that, I remember. We were doing a night scene, it was snowing and we had to climb a twenty-foot wall, the three of us that were escaping – Percy Herbert, Jack Rodney and me. And Charlie. We had this vast ladder and we had to pick it up, push it against the wall and run up it. On the other side of the wall was a scaffolding built up to about five feet from the top that we jumped on to. I was terrified and I think Jack was and Percy might have been scared as well, but he didn't show it. We could only shoot it once because it was very late and it

was nearly getting light. Peter Graham Scott, who was the director, said, "We have to get this shot and we've only got one go at it." So we ran up the ladder and Percy jumped over the top and Jack went next and I was the last one to go up. I got to the top and I looked over and Jack and Percy was shouting, "Don't jump!" because the scaffolding was swaying from side to side. But I had to go, and I did and, God, it was frightening! So much in films happens like that because it's thrown together. You're working against a schedule all the time. You find that all the time.'

So much in comedy is fate, coincidence, that in retrospect you find yourself asking a number of 'What ifs?' What if Mrs Marx had had girls? What if Eric's mum hadn't spotted a teenage Ernie? What if solicitor Bob Mortimer hadn't been drunk enough to heckle Vic Reeves that night in a pub in south London? And what if Ronnie Barker, West End actor and semi-known televisual face, hadn't popped in one night for a drink at the Buckstone, an actors' drinking club just off Shaftesbury Avenue? He might never have met the bartender, a between-jobs Scottish performer who shared a forename with Mr Barker.

Ronnie Corbett hailed from Edinburgh. He met Ronnie Barker by serving him a drink. They spent a few moments talking about this and that, actors shooting the breeze. Both, of course, had no idea that in a few short years upwards of 20 million people would be doing the same thing with them on a weekly basis. 'It was a theatrical club. You could have lunch and dinner there and the bar could be said to be open till about 3.30am,' recalls Ronnie B. 'It should have closed at 11 but it was one of those sort of places that I think the police didn't bother with. It wasn't sleazy, it was just an actors' drinking club and the actors just carried on drinking halfway through the night. And I used to go in there and there he was behind the bar. He had a little part-time job there. And that's where I met him first. Then, he was just the man who was serving. I knew who he was, I knew he was an actor, but we didn't become chums then.'

It wasn't that big an event, of course, but Ronnie Corbett remembers it equally vividly: 'He was doing quite a lot of radio shows like *The Navy Lark* at that time. I don't think we thought

found himself back on radio with his close friend Leslie Crowther as a regular player (alongside *Seven Faces Of Jim* alumnus June Whitfield) in *Crowther's Crowd*. The three had previously worked as a trio on *Variety Playhouse* and *Radio Times* described this new show thus: 'They are three students out to reform the world – Leslie the medical student, June the drama student and Ronnie a trainee at a school for chefs. Thanks to the miracle of radio, listeners can join their

'He was behind **THE BAR**. He had a little **PART-TIME** job there. And that's where I met him first. Then, he was **JUST THE MAN** who was **SERVING**. I knew who he was, I knew he was an actor, but we didn't become **CHUMS** then.'

ON MEETING RONNIE CORBETT

about it in any momentous way but we knew each other a bit because I had worked with his wife Joy in a pantomime in Bromley where she was the stage manager. So I'd known her before and she was with him when he used to come down for supper sometimes.' It would be three years before the paths of the two Ronnies crossed again, becoming inextricably linked.

Following a brief appearance in *Doctor In Distress* – 'I had one line. I came up behind James Robertson Justice. He sneezed. I said. "That's a nasty cold, you should see a doctor." He said. "I am a doctor!" That was it.' – Ronnie

summit conferences at El Aroma coffee bar in Bloomsbury... they'll argue about anything and illustrate their points with impersonations.' June Whitfield adds: 'It was really a sort of continuation from *Variety Playhouse*. We were very much a team at that time, but people drift on to different things so that was to be the end of that, sadly.'

The movie *Father Came Too* not only saw Ronnie reunited with Leslie Phillips, Stanley Baxter and James Robertson Justice, but also provided another blueprint for the future role of Norman Stanley Fletcher.

In **Father Came Too** *with* **Leslie Phillips (middle) and Stanley Baxter, 1963.**

Another movie, the dialogue-free *A Home Of Your Own*, was to prove equally influential. 'I play the man who was laying the cement and everyone kept going over it, running over it. I fell into it. I had this great sequence where I suddenly threw everything down and I danced on it. I did ballet steps, I did swimming, I did everything in it. There again, you could only do everything once because of the costume. That was all done on a shoestring as well but it gave me an idea. Having seen it I thought, "These silent things really work. I should do this." So *Futtock's End* was the first [in 1970] and it was directed by Bob Kellett, who also directed *A Home Of Your Own*. I got him because he'd also directed this one.' Further filmic opportunities were offered up by *The Bargee*, ostensibly a Galton and Simpson vehicle for their *Steptoe And Son* star Harry H Corbett. 'I suppose that was the biggest part I played, because I played Harry Corbett's cousin who ran the narrow boats. We had ten weeks on the narrow boats. I had to have my hair dyed black to match Harry's. Eric Sykes was in that as well. Hugh Griffiths was a sort of heavy and I remember we rehearsed a scene where I was trying to get him drunk to

keep him out of the house while Harry Corbett had it away with his daughter. But he eventually drank me under the table. I said some line and burped in the rehearsal and Hugh looked at me and said, "You gonna burp there?" I said. "Yes." So we did the take and about two lines before I burped, he burped. I said, "You knew I was going to burp there." He said."I know, but I just felt it, it just came out." Bloody liar! But he was a very good liar.'

Brian Wilde, who would later play prison officer Barrowclough in *Porridge,* also appeared in the movie. Ronnie's work on television in 1964 was also to prove instrumental in his career. Eric Sykes was one of the first comics of his generation who, along with the likes of Tony Hancock and Benny Hill, realised the full potential of television. By this time, Sykes was a medium mainstay, with a series of shows designed to showcase his talents in sitcom format.

Displaying his penchant for playing older characters, Ronnie guested as a hard-to-lose old tramp in one episode of the show, *Sykes And The Log Cabin*. 'People say, "How do you find characters like that?" And you can never answer them. The only answer is that it's your job and you get used to it. It's the same with playing an old man, I suppose. I never made a study of it. All through my life I've never consciously studied people to get characters but obviously a lot of it rubs off on you subconsciously. You pick it up without knowing it. You look at the old chaps in a pub and you suddenly get a character.'

It was while working on *Sykes* that Ronnie first met a young BBC producer and director

With Hugh Griffiths in **The Bargee,** *1964.*

by the name of Sydney Lotterby. Lotterby would go on to perform those duties for Ronnie on *Porridge*, *Open All Hours* and *The Magnificent Evans*.

TV Or Not TV?

By 1965, Ronnie Barker was a known figure on both television and radio, with what appeared to be a blossoming film career, albeit in supporting roles. Having worked in these media, he was beginning to realise which one he felt most comfortable in. 'Television was my market place. I think I thought that's where I should be. Television is the only place where you can get series. You don't get series of films. You don't say, "Oh I've got a good film series, I'm doing *Terminator 1, 2, 3* and *4*." You do a film at a time. I also knew it was a much bigger market. Television was somehow more parochial, more cosy. I never had vaulting ambition, as they say in "the Scottish play". I just loved working and I

wanted to be successful, I wanted to earn money. I wanted to be well known. So I thought, "Television." It's British, for a start, and I've never thought of anything outside Britain really as being my métier at all. I thought, "If you make it big here..." Films were lovely if they came along and, fine, I would do them. But television seemed to be the thing to work at. The thing to conquer and, touch wood, I think I managed it.'

So it was to television that Ronnie Barker devoted himself, appearing in a variety of roles, from Spettigue in a production of rep favourite *Charley's Aunt*, toplining Danny LaRue ('Danny looked wonderful and he played it very well, although I felt he was miscast. He would only play it as a beautiful woman, which doesn't quite fit the thing. It should be a little rugby player.') to that of Jerry Cruncher in the BBC's Sunday afternoon adaptation of Charles Dickens' *A Tale Of Two Cities*. 'I was a bank messenger but I was also a grave robber. And I remember saying to Joan Craft,

'**TELEVISION** *seemed to be
the thing to work at.* **THE THING** *to conquer
and, touch wood, I think* **I MANAGED IT**'

who was the director, "I've summed this character up – he doesn't know whether to take the money or open the box." She couldn't understand that for a bit, of course that was the great catchphrase of the quiz show *Take Your Pick*.'

Having co-starred with Cyril Fletcher in the radio comedy *Not To Worry*, Ronnie was rewarded with his first top billing in the 1965 show, *Let's Face It*. 'It was because I was in *Not To Worry* and the director John Fawcett Wilson took a shine to me and he suggested they should do a series for me as well. It was a run-of-the-mill sketch show, written by everybody. By today's standards I wouldn't want it to be heard now. There are very few things I feel that about. I don't even feel it about *The Navy Lark*, because that was quite good stuff, quite fruity, meaty stuff. Very broad comedy, but good lines. But I should think *Let's Face It* was very run-of-the-mill. I remember a lot of puns. I had to keep cutting out puns. It was OK, and it certainly gave

me the first top billing.'

Headlining roles also came along on television courtesy of *Gaslight Theatre*. The show was based around a touring Victorian repertory company who each week performed classic melodramas, live on BBC2. Adapted by Alec Clunes, the six hour-long shows also featured Warren Mitchell, Alfred Marks and Patricia Routledge, among others, and gave Ronnie the opportunity to play everything from 'an American dastard' to a 'a revolting Dutch miner' to 'Shawnegenwam', a Red Indian in the wonderfully-titled *The Blood-Craz'd Scourge Of The Redskin Wilderness, Or What You Will*. 'I was supposed to be the manager of the company. There was no backstage to it so none of this was known. It was simply presenting these melodramas. But they were done live to an audience and at one point I was playing the old Gypsy, Ishmail Lee, in *Maria Marten* and thirty seconds later I was playing his son, who was a

'**I STOOD UP** – *I've never done this before or since, and Warren* **MITCHELL** *always remembers it – and said, "OK, Alec, it's two hours.* **WHEN** *it's an hour, give us a ring and I'll come in again." And I walked out. I was* **AMAZED** *at my own courage*'

blond. It was the same man in that the manager was playing both parts so I had to do this costume and make-up change in 30 seconds. On stage, this crowd gathered round the gypsy and chanted and wailed and I was off changing. It was all wonderful. They had models like they had in Victorian times. There was a chase across the rooftops in *Maria Marten* and they had a series of puppets and rooftops going into the distance. The policeman chased this man off stage and downstage on came these puppets that went across stage, then smaller puppets came across and then tiny puppets came across.

It was very funny. Alec Clunes also said – he was a great historian on these things – that they used to use modern songs, even if they were doing something in, say, 1870 and it was supposed to take place in 1750, it would still have modern 1870 music hall songs in it as well. Like a panto, I suppose. So, of course, we were singing things like *Hot Time In The Old Town Tonight*. In one of the plays I played a Welsh Red Indian and also a sort of James Cagney cowboy. He had a blond curly wig as well. I looked hopelessly mutton dressed as lamb. We did one called *The Worst Woman In London* in which I played Lord

Stir-crazy in The Cracksman *with Percy Herbert and Charlie Drake, 1963.*

Rustless, really. It was a wonderful part. I sang *A Bachelor Gay Am I*, which was quite anachronistic.'

Gaslight Theatre was also to provoke Ronnie into an uncharacteristic display of temperament. 'Alec Clunes would come in on the first day and we would read this hour-long piece and it would come in at two hours. Then he'd say, "I'll come in tomorrow morning with cuts." Then he'd come in the next morning and we would read these cuts which were like, "Don't say, 'I've never been so disgusted in my life.' Say, 'I'm disgusted.' " And we'd read it all again and we'd find it lasted one hour 50 minutes. This happened for three weeks and eventually, in the fourth week, we read it and it came to two hours. And I stood up – I've never done this before or since, and Warren Mitchell always remembers it – and said, "OK, Alec, it's two hours. When it's an hour, give us a ring and I'll come in again." And I walked out. I was amazed at my own courage. I remember their faces as I went out. They were frozen. Even Alfred Marks didn't have anything to say, which is very unusual. Warren said afterwards, "I don't know how you did that, but it worked." The same evening Alec rang me up and said, "Ronnie, you're absolutely right. It's no use going on like this. Why don't you cut it?" So I said, "OK. I'll cut it." And this particular piece had a subplot which ran all the way through and Bill Owen and Megs Jenkins were cast. But it had nothing to do with the rest of the play, so I cut them right out, rang Alec and said, "Megs and Bill have gone completely. Is that OK? Can you tell them?" They went and it was down to about an hour and ten minutes, so I cut another ten minutes and it was OK. After that he used to say, "Will you cut them?" I enjoyed that and it was comparatively easy.'

Working on the scripts for *Gaslight Theatre* was the first time Ronnie had put pen to paper since his days with Glenn Melvyn. Yet he instinctively knew how to make things work, a talent that would eventually see him involved in most of the material he subsequently played. Ronnie has often spoken of his fondness for old gags – 'As I've always said, old jokes are only old jokes if you've heard them before. You can have a joke from 1895 and if you haven't heard it before it's a new joke to you. It has to be funny, and so often they aren't. But some of them are. That's what it is. I find it's universal. If a joke is funny it stays funny forever' – and his next screen venture gave him plenty of opportunity to exploit that fondness.

Before The Fringe was a show based around old-time music hall jokes and sketches, many of which were performed by Ronnie in tandem with Beryl Reid. The show's title deliberately referred to the stage revue *Beyond The Fringe*, the 1960 production featuring the combined talents of Peter Cook, Dudley Moore, Jonathan Miller and Alan Bennett that had turned British comedy on its head. In *Before The Fringe*, Ronnie Barker paid tribute to what had gone before. But it would be a graduate of the so-called Oxbridge comedy Mafia, a man who owed his career to both the comedic and indeed social advancements made by the *Beyond The Fringe* troupe, who would finally make a star out of Ronnie Barker. ⊙⊙

Ronnie with his mentor Glenn Melvyn, as the Fastest Gun in Finchley, *an episode of* The Ronnie Barker Playhouse, *1968.*

Chapter THREE

Hello, Good Evening And Welcome To The Big Time

DAVID Frost was something of a phenomenon. While his Cambridge contemporary Peter Cook was leading the British 'satire boom' at his London night club The Establishment, Frost was packaging it wholesale and serving it up to the mainstream via television. As the frontman of both *That Was The Week That Was* (*TW3*) and *Not So Much A Programme, More A Way Of Life*,

Street and David was stepping out with a girl in the show called Jenny Logan. So he used to come in there quite a lot and saw me. Ronnie B was a lot better known than either John or I.'

Not sharing the university background of Frost and Cleese, the two Ronnies naturally drifted together. 'That's when Ronnie C and I teamed up, because they were all a bit university there and we were grammar school boys. Everyone goes to university now, but 30 years ago university was sort of a cut above. They were

> '*There was* **NO ENMITY** *or no real distance, but if you had to group together in twos, naturally* **RONNIE AND I** *would go together as John and David did*'

he had established himself as a unique force in British television, equally comfortable whether cracking gags or interviewing leading politicians.

In March 1966 he launched his new series, *The Frost Report*, an irreverent look at one particular topic each week. The show featured a number of sketches and for this Frost assembled a team of three – John Cleese, Ronnie Corbett and Ronnie Barker. 'David Frost brought me along,' recalls Ronnie Corbett. 'He had seen me quite a lot in night clubs. I was in a show with Barry Cryer at a club called Winston's in Clifford

a bit grand, especially John Cleese, who was very grand. He was nice, but nevertheless we felt that he and David – they were them and we were us. There was no enmity or no real distance, but if you had to group together in twos, naturally Ronnie and I would go together as John and David did.' 'That linked us, that's true,' agrees Corbett. 'Also the fact that we were much more experienced theatrical performers than both of them, Ronnie in particular. I think it's also funny that both Ronnie and I were brought up and raised in big university towns, Oxford and

'I look down on him...' Ronnie Corbett, Ronnie Barker and John Cleese, a class apart in the famous sketch from The Frost Report, *1966.*

Edinburgh, with the university glowering over both of us, although we didn't attend it. So there was a comfort thing between us.'

In retrospect, *The Frost Report* can be seen as a hugely important breeding ground for modern British comedy. It indirectly begat *Monty Python's Flying Circus* (Graham Chapman, Eric Idle, Terry Jones and Michael Palin all wrote for the show) and it put the two Ronnies together for the first time, beginning an on-screen partnership that would last for another two decades. The show, which ran for two seasons, produced numerous classic sketches, perhaps the most famous of which remains John Law's biting take on class, personified by the distinct difference in height of the three central performers, with the tall Cleese playing Upper Class, the medium Barker personifying Middle Class and the diminutive Corbett as the flat capped Working Class. 'You could put a plank down between Ronnie Corbett's head and John Cleese's head and my head would touch it as well. We were absolutely in a straight line. So they thought Upper Class, Middle Class, Lower Class and that's where the whole "I look up to him," "I look down on him," came from. That was the whole premise of the sketch, because there weren't funny lines in it. I wrote about three others, about work and other things, trying to get more laughs in them, more jokes, because I couldn't use the looking up or looking down because we'd done that. But that's the one that everyone remembers and I sort of wish they didn't show that one so much. I wish they'd show something else, but probably not much of *The Frost Report* still exists at all. I remember John doing the funny walks thing, before *Python*, before the Ministry Of Silly Walks. He did that first in *The Frost Report*.'

Although Frost was closely associated with the satire boom, *The Frost Report* had less of a biting social edge than his previous shows. '*TW3* and *Not So Much A Programme, More A Way Of Life* were political programmes. Ours may have appeared to be a topical and pointed show, but in fact it wasn't. I think it was just humour. You see the things that David read out on the clipboard, that we later did as news items in *The Two Ronnies*. They may have sounded topical, but they weren't at all topical. People used to say that in *The Two Ronnies* we sat there and we did all those topical jokes. And I'd say, "You pick one topical joke there. There isn't one." That's why you can show them 20 years later and they're not dated, except you might get "the Prime Minister Harold Wilson..." or something. We shouldn't even have done that at the time but we did. But the jokes were not to do with current affairs at all. And I think that *The Frost Report* may have given that impression but it wasn't.'

The Frost Report not only gave Ronnie B his first on-screen experience with Ronnie C, it also allowed him to develop what would become one of his trademarks in *The Two Ronnies* – the monologue. 'John Cleese started by doing monologues. He was like the headmaster talking to his pupils and so on. And there was one, as the Chancellor of the Exchequer, which John couldn't do for some reason and Jimmy Gilbert said. "Let Ronnie do this one for a change." And, of course, I never looked back. I always did all the monologues straight through *The Two Ronnies*, all those spokesmen. That started there by accident because John couldn't do it. 'Often the three of us were in sketches together. Sometimes there were two people in a sketch and sometimes I would do a sketch with John Cleese. It wasn't a fixed thing, it wasn't that any two-handed sketches were done by the two Ronnies. Usually, they tried to write for three people.'

Shortly before beginning his stint on *The Frost Report*, Ronnie appeared with two other products of the Fringe, Peter Cook and Dudley Moore, in *Not Only... But Also...* A hugely inventive sketch show, *Not Only...* probably showcased the talents of Cook and Moore better than anything in their subsequent careers and each week featured a guest who would take part in the regular feature, Poets Cornered. Pete, Dud and said guest – in this instance, Ronnie Barker – sat suspended over a tank of gunge and

to the mast", and I was going to add, "I shall not turn around, he said 'till Oscar Wilde has passed." And I got as far as his back glued to the mast and I said, "I shall not..." and the button went so I went in. I was furious, but I'd arranged to take my glasses off when I went in, so I came up and said, "I've lost my glasses." Dudley was so distraught he jumped in with me. Afterwards, I said to Jimmy Gilbert, who was directing, "Jimmy, I thought you pushed the button when you stumbled or failed to deliver. I was going great guns, I was about to give you a laugh." He replied, "We always drop the guest in first and I

'John Cleese did the *FUNNY WALKS* thing, before *PYTHON*, before the Ministry of Silly Walks. He did that first in The *FROST* Report'

attempted to speak in rhyming couplets. 'And whenever the bell went the next person had to take over. So he would say, "As I was going down the road one dark and windy day, I saw a man the other side..." and then the button would go and someone else would carry on. And it was frightening because it was completely unscripted and unrehearsed and you were trying desperately to make this rhyme and terrified of going into this unknown pool. And, of course, Peter Cook was so clever that he would try to involve you in a risqué rhyme. I suddenly remembered a line I had heard somewhere before, and tried to get it in. I was about to say, "The cabin boy stood fearlessly, his back glued

thought it had gone on long enough." I was furious. But it was a wonderful experience and afterwards we went up to their usual haunt in Hampstead for a party. I enjoyed the evening very much. They were great lads.'

Purrrfect Casting

In between appearing on *The Frost Report*, Ronnie was being kept extremely busy by a number of other appearances; in two films for the Children's Film Foundation, *Runaway Railway* and *Ghost Of A Chance*, and guest star turns in two of television's most popular dramas, *The Saint* and *The Avengers*.

The Saint episode saw Ronnie tipping the

Ronnie in his first sitcom, Foreign Affairs, *1966.*

nod to Jacques Tati in his role as a clumsy French detective, while *The Avengers* episode, *The Hidden Tiger*, saw Ronnie cast as a mysterious cat fancier named Cheshire. The character could almost have been a forerunner of the numerous spokesmen he later played on *The Two Ronnies*, as Cheshire was the head of PURRR – The Philanthropic Union For The Rescue, Relief And Recuperation Of Cats.

Another television appearance holds less happy memories for Ronnie. His old friend Leslie Crowther had asked him to appear on his popular children's show, *Crackerjack*, the same week that his son Laurence was taken ill with measles. 'I went to do the programme on the Monday and when I got home my son was much worse. The doctor had come and said he had pneumonia. So he was rushed into the hospital and put in an oxygen tent and I sat there all night. At one point, the nurse couldn't change the oxygen and I had to summon up the strength of ten men to open the new oxygen tank. I got home in the early morning – I remember this so vividly – and by the time Friday came and the show was being shown, my son, who had been so looking forward to seeing me on Crackerjack, was in the oxygen tent and I was sitting next to his bed. The programme was showing in the ward and I came on. And I cried. I remember crying and thinking, "Poor little sod, he was looking forward to this and now look at him." But he came through all right. I did a little drawing of him, he was getting better but he was still in the tent, and I've still got it, his little wan face was so thin... It was a very, very moving moment, thinking if he's not going to survive this and he was so looking forward to seeing me on *Crackerjack* and there it is on and he can't even see it. That was very upsetting for me.'

A new series, *Foreign Affairs*, offered Ronnie his first stab at proper weekly situation comedy. Debuting on 8 September, 1966 (shortly after the end of *The Frost Report*'s first run) and written by Johnnie Mortimer and Brian Cooke, the show was based around the exploits of the Foreign Office's Dennis Proudfoot, played by *Navy Lark* regular Leslie Phillips. Ronnie played the role of Russian Ambassador Grischa Petrovitch, Proudfoot's chess-playing opposite number. 'I remember Frank Muir, who was head of light entertainment at the BBC at the time, came up to me and said, "We've got this idea we think you'd be right for." I remember them coming on to the stage when we were doing *The Frost Report* at the Shepherd's Bush Empire, and saying Leslie Phillips wants to do it and you know him, and we think you could play the Russian. So I was pleased with that because it was a step forward. And it was fun to do it with Leslie because he's a very funny man and I'd worked so long with him in *The Navy Lark* so I knew his every move and he knew mine.'

Although ostensibly it dealt with Cold War issues, the emphasis was firmly on Phillips' girl chasing and the show was not exactly a classic, lasting just the one brief six-week run.

1967's *The Man Outside* was probably as close to Hollywood as Ronnie Barker ever got. It starred Hollywood's very own (yet improbably named) Van Heflin and was distributed in America. Ronnie's role was confined to the movie's first reel, but for that time he shared the screen alone with Heflin, picking up a few tips on screen acting along the way. 'He was a real, real pro. Knew everything. He said, "Ronnie, don't ever take a drag on a cigarette in a close up and don't ever take a drink in a close-up." I said. "Why not?" And he said, "They will

Ronnie with U.S. movie star Van Heflin, learning how to smoke in The Man Outside, *1967.*

never be able to edit it because you will not be doing exactly the same thing in the other shot and you will lose the close-up. If you do that, your close-up will not be in. And I used to watch him and he never did. Very clever. I just loved that. That was a taste of the American movies really. My only one.'

successful mix of Frost's ever developing clipboard-grasping monologues, as well as comedy sketches. Cleese had tired of performing and opted out this time round, leaving room for the occasional appearance of writer Michael Palin. 'John wanted to write and he was getting a bit nervous of performing as well. He used to

'People have been **ACCUSED**, not only us, but lots of people, of using the same **PEOPLE** all the time. And the reason is you know you can **RELY ON THEM**. You don't have to worry about them. And you've only got a few days to rehearse and they can only **DO IT ONCE** and it's got to be right'

A Paradine Of Its Former Self

The second series of *The Frost Report* proved even more successful than the first, picking up the Golden Rose Of Montreux. As adept as he was before the camera, David Frost was equally skilled in the business side of making television. His own Paradine Productions took charge of the show and its principal performers were also signed to Paradine, effectively ensuring Frost's involvement with Ronnie up until the fifth season of *The Two Ronnies*. One of Frost's more astute moves was to relocate to the 'other side', commercial television. Here, the programme morphed into *Frost On Sunday*, an equally

be very white and pale and worried before he went on *The Frost Report* and he said, "I don't really like performing, I'd rather write," and so that's when he left.'

Another addition to the cast was Josephine Tewson, with whom Ronnie was then co-starring in the West End production of Tom Stoppard's *The Real Inspector Hound*. 'The two Ronnies were doing the sketches and they had to have somebody else there to play the woman,' Josephine Tewson explains. 'So when they needed a girl, and a versatile one at that, Ronnie said. "Well, there's this girl and she's playing Mrs Drudge. As she's got to be there during the week doing the play, she's going to be available on Sunday." And so it went on. And when the play came off they then put me under contract. I got to know Ronnie quite well just going backwards and forwards from Wembley Park, where the studios were, to the theatre.' 'She was just very good in that play,' says Barker, 'a good character woman. And that's why we had her in *Frost On Sunday*. You've got to have someone you can rely on and I was always on the look-out for someone who knew their lines the next day in rehearsals. And Jo was the same, she knows what she's doing. And you do work with people you know because you haven't got time to experiment, ever, with those sort of things. People have been accused, not just us, lots of people, of using the same people all the time. And the reason is you know you can rely on them. You don't have to worry about them. And you've only got a few days to rehearse and they can only do it once and it's got to be right. It would be lovely to try different people in different things but you haven't got the luxury of that because it's on television and you're as good as your supporting cast. If you're very good and everyone else is rotten, the show will be rotten.'

Jo Tewson recalls one telling conversation she had with Ronnie as they waited for the tube to get them to their performance of *The Real Inspector Hound*. 'The train was late and I thought we might miss the half-hour call at the Criterion that night and I said, "Well, the show must go on." "Why?" he said. "Why must the show go on?" "Well it must," I said. "No, no, no, Jo. Nobody's going to bother if we're not there. The world's not going to come to an end if we don't do the show tonight." That's anathema to me but he's not like that at all. He is so balanced.

I remember while we were doing *Frost On Sunday* he was offered a good Shakespearean part on BBC2, something you give your eye teeth to play and something he hadn't done before. He was saying, "Oh, isn't it a pity? They've offered me this but I can't do it because it's during the school holidays." And I said, "What do you mean you can't do it during the school holidays?" and he said, "I always go down to Littlehampton with Joy and the kids." And I was thinking, "There are trains, Ronnie," and he just said. "No, I don't do this during the school holidays." He was totally balanced. He knew the value of having his wife and children and he knew he had to have this holiday. I think that's marvellous. He'd absolutely got it right and very few actors do.'

Wiley By Name

Frost On Sunday was an hour-long show which featured around five sketches of approximately two minutes in length. Ronnie felt that, despite boasting one of the most impressive writing teams in all of television, the material was not always as strong as it could be. And thus was a man named Gerald Wiley born. 'I remember going to David at the end of one show, and it hadn't gone well, but David was always so optimistic. He said, "What a wonderful show · that was." And I said, "No. It was bloody dreadful, David. It was terrible and the scripts were awful." Ronnie Corbett looked at me and thought, "My God! He's sticking his neck out here. He could be out on his ear." But I felt I had to say it. We must somehow do better that this. 'So I went home and I thought, people aren't writing stuff for us. So I decided I would write something. I had a couple of ideas and I decided I would write them and send them in under an assumed name. I spoke to my agent and he said,

Ronnie as a monk in **Talk of Angels,** *from* **Ronnie Barker Playhouse, 1968. With Liz Crowther.**

"Well, you'll have to send them through me. I'll have to pretend I'm this man's agent as well." So I picked this name Gerald Wiley, because I thought most people, when they have a pseudonym, always have a glamorous name like Rock Armstrong or something wonderful. So I picked a really ugly name that no one would dream of picking as their pseudonym. Gerald Wiley – that's a really ugly name. Then I said, "Supposing they want to see me?" And my agent said, "I'll tell them you're a bit of a recluse, an older man, I'll say, but you've seen the shows and thought you might try your hand." So in came the scripts and the producer said, "I've got two new scripts in from another writer, must be something to do with David I suppose, a man named Wiley." And we laughed, and I laughed, and we sat and read the scripts and he said, "What do you think?" Ronnie C said, "Well, they're not bad. I think we ought to try them." So we tried them. Secretly, I was very pleased. So for the next three weeks we did sketches by Gerald Wiley, as well as other sketches.'

Ronnie had chosen to work under a

pseudonym so that the cast and crew would be brutally honest over the material and not try to cushion the performer/writer's ego. He found out how well this worked in the fourth week when Wiley's material was deemed to be well below par by all those concerned. 'I was pleased, really, because that was exactly what I wanted. I wanted complete anonymity. I wanted people to choose them only if they liked them. If, for instance, Ronnie Corbett came up and said, "I've written this sketch," and you didn't like it you'd say, "It's

"Well, he let us down there, didn't he?" and I was defending him, "Be fair. He's done so many." '

Keeping Wiley a secret from the rest of the Frost crew was leading Ronnie to ridiculous lengths, at one point instructing his agent to appease Frank Muir's desire to know more by setting up a meeting, then later calling back to cancel it.

Ronnie C was also eager to know more about Wiley and was keen to buy the rights to some of his sketches so he could use them in his act. He

> 'I picked this name **GERALD WILEY**, because I thought most people when they have a **PSEUDONYM**, they always have a glamorous name like Rock Armstrong or something wonderful. So I picked a really ugly name that **NO ONE WOULD DREAM** of picking as their pseudonym. Gerald Wiley – that's a really ugly name'

very good, Ron. It's excellent," while knowing you didn't want to do it. I thought I couldn't have that. So that's why I kept it up. I kept it up through the whole of the first series and the series was about 26 episodes long, a long series. I kept it up all the time. And sometimes they were rejected but most were done.' 'One sketch was about a ventriloquist,' recalls Ronnie Corbett 'and it really died, the first Gerald Wiley to go down the pan. When we came off Ronnie said,

unknowingly contacted his colleague via the agent, an opportunity that Ronnie B couldn't help but exploit. 'We did a sketch called the Doctor's Waiting Room which featured Ronnie almost entirely and he wanted to do it in a summer show, because he used to do summer shows and pantos. And he said, "Do you think he'll sell it to me?" So I said, "Write to him, you know he's with my agent, anyway." So the agent said, "I've had this letter from Ronnie Corbett

Ronnie B 'marrying' Ronnie C and Josephine Tewson in **Frost On Sunday,** *1968.*

saying can he buy the sketch?" I said "Charge him £250 for it." A few days later, Ronnie came in and said, "He wants £250 for it," so I told him, "That's rubbish. Don't pay it. It's not worth that." Anyway, it was Christmas time and I said to my agent, "Send it to Ronnie Corbett and say Mr Wiley would be very grateful if you would accept this sketch with his compliments, free of charge, because you've done such marvellous work with his sketches and made them look so

funny on screen." And Ronnie came to me and said, "He's given it to me, he's given me the sketch." I said, "Oh, that's nice of him." So a short while later, half a dozen crystal goblets arrived from Ronnie Corbett, all inscribed with the initials 'GW' for "all the many sketches you've given me and for giving me that sketch." Of course, I took them and said, "Well, thanks for the glasses, Ronnie," afterwards.'

As Ronnie Corbett confirms, after a while the

Frost crew began to doubt the existence of Wiley, convinced that he must be another writer. 'I suppose it was a comment and a judgement of how good the material was, that is must have been written by an expert. We knew it wasn't written by somebody who'd just started writing. There was more than a bit of quality about it. Somebody ran a book to try and guess who he was. The most illustrious names were in there – Tom Stoppard, Noel Coward was still alive so his name was down there, Rattigan, Willis Hall, Keith Waterhouse, Frank Muir. Given that it came through his agent, Ronnie B used to visualise this character as being possibly a novelist or short-story writer or playwright, possibly gay, so that was the rumour he put out. And we all fed on it.'

Wiley's true identity could remain a secret no longer. 'So I wrote a letter – I had Wiley notepaper printed and everything – saying that Gerald Wiley would like to entertain the cast of *Frost On Sunday* at the Chinese restaurant opposite the studio. So all the writers turned up as well because there were bets going on as to who he was. And it said Gerald Wiley would be there to meet you. Then the time came and Frank Muir was late. I was there already and Frank Muir came in and they all applauded him as he entered, and he said, "It's not me, it's not me." And when everyone was there I got up and said, "Can I just say something before we start? It's me. I'm Gerald Wiley." And David Frost said. "It *is* you. I wondered about that." He was the only one. It was out then. From that moment I wished it hadn't been out because with *The Two Ronnies* I was writing stuff and they were saying. "Ooh, that's very good," so I was back in the situation I didn't want to be in. If it had continued all my life it would've been better.'

In many ways, it did continue for all of Ronnie's life. Gerald Wiley lived on as a writer for *The Two Ronnies*, penning the vast majority of their serials. Other pseudonyms – Jonathan Cobbold, Jack Goetz, Dave Huggett and Larry Keith, Bob Ferris – all graced the works of Ronnie Barker. All were, of course, Ronnie himself. 'They were just used for the public, because everyone in the biz knew it was me. You see, I don't like "Produced by Charlie Chaplin, music by Charlie Chaplin, starring Charlie Chaplin." Or Orson Welles. Orson Welles and Charlie Chaplin would put their names on things five times if they could. So that's why I used other names, just to put the ordinary punter off, who didn't really care who wrote a thing. I didn't really want to put my name on things more than once.'

Showbiz partnerships are often referred to as a marriage. The 'marriage' between Ronnie B and Ronnie C lasted for 22 years. In all that time, you'd expect there to have been arguments, falling outs, negotiations, reconciliations.

According to both men, this was never the case. It was a good, strong marriage, kept alive no doubt by the fact that they always had parallel, and equally successful, solo careers. They never fell out, although they came close once, when Ronnie C had been picked as a candidate for *This Is Your Life*.

During work on *Frost On Sunday*, a sketch appeared that featured an ordinary man who was convinced that he was going to be on *This Is Your Life*. He was so certain they were going to get him that he wouldn't leave the house. Eventually the payoff comes when he heads off for a drink with his best mate – played by Eamonn Andrews, then the host of the popular show.

They asked Andrews to appear on the sketch but he declined. Weeks later, when Frost and Co

'Ronnie used to *VISUALISE* this character *WILEY* as being possibly a novelist or short story writer or playwright, *POSSIBLY GAY*, so that was the *RUMOUR* he put out. And we all fed on it'

RONNIE CORBETT

were surreptitiously approached by the *This Is Your Life* people, Ronnie B suggested using the sketch as a means to nab an unsuspecting Ronnie C. 'It was the last of the series and they said this couldn't be better. Then we went in, the producer Phil Casson and I in cahoots, and said to Ronnie, "As it's the end of the series I thought we might try Eamonn again. I think he might do it because it's the end of the series and he owes David a few favours." So Ronnie said, "Fine, fine." But Ronnie was already cast in another sketch, because one of us played the good part and one of us played the feed part, we swapped round. But Phil said, "As you're going to play the lead in the Eamonn Andrews sketch, Ronnie B will have to play the lead in the sketch you've been rehearsing." Now, that was a sketch that Ronnie C was very fond of. He thought that somehow this was a trick to get him. He lost confidence or something.'

'He fiddled me into a role that was palpably not right for me,' confirms Corbett, 'and took that role for himself. So I thought, for the first time, "Now, this is a mistake. I should be playing that role and it is funnier. He's trying to do something

funny here." And I walked out of the room and came home and said to my wife, Anne, "I'm being manipulated and I don't think it's right." '

'It was the only moment that we've ever had that was slightly worrying for him,' says Ronnie B. 'Not for me because I knew what we were up to. But he sort of became distanced from me a bit. He said, "Why are they doing this?" And his wife said, "Oh, ride it out. You're doing so well together, the both of you, I'm sure he's not doing that." So he was a bit distant but he did it. We were friends, alright. It wasn't a tiff or anything but I could feel a little distancing. So came the day and we were sitting there all ready and geared up and Ronnie C went out to the canteen or something and came back and said, "There are Thames Television vans everywhere." And I thought, "Oh, Christ! Why have they showed themselves?" But I said, "What does that mean?" He said, "Well, I wonder if it's a *This Is Your Life*?" I said, "It must be David Frost. I'll go and find out." So I went outside and saw the vans there and walked about for five minutes and went back and said, "It is. It's David. The rumour is that it's David Frost." And Ronnie said, "Of

'He *FIDDLED* me into a role that was palpably *NOT RIGHT FOR ME* and took that role for himself. So I thought for the first time, now this is a *MISTAKE*'

RONNIE CORBETT

course, it could be one of us," and that was the best moment I've ever had of thinking on my feet, I said, "No, it couldn't be one of us." Ronnie said, "Why not?" "Because the other one would know." And he said, "Oh, yeah. Well, that's a relief." It was like the sword of Damocles. I thought I must say something and he fell for it straight away. If he'd thought about it, of course, he could've said, "Well, perhaps you do know," but he didn't. And then it was such a surprise. You could see it on the screen. He turns to me and says, "You bastard," which is, I think, the most frequent word ever used on *This Is Your Life*. They usually turn to somebody and say, "You bastard." That was wonderful. It was one of my proudest moments for thinking on my feet.'

Years later, plans to feature Ronnie B on the show would be scuppered when he found a piece of paper his wife had left lying around with an unknown phone number on. He dialled the number and was put through to a researcher for *This Is Your Life*.

While working on *The Bargee* back in 1964, Ronnie had suddenly decided to spend his time between set ups writing a mock Edwardian music-hall song. He showed the lyrics to writers Galton and Simpson, who were encouraging. The song was titled *Not Too Tall, Not Too Short*, and in the intervening years Ronnie penned a few more, such titles as *They Tell Me There's A Lot Of It About*, *Billy Pratt's Bananas* and *The Black Pudding March*. During his stint on *Frost On Sunday*, Ronnie showed some of these to Laurie Holloway, the show's musical arranger, who suggested they work on the music together and turn it into an album. The result was *A Pint Of Old And Filthy*. 'The title sort of indicates that some of them are old and some of them are filthy, or both. And I don't know how successful they were, but they were published and I enjoyed it very much. A couple of people have asked if they can do the numbers in their act.'

Eager to increase his hold on all things televisual, David Frost spun each of his *Frost*

Ronnie in Tennyson, *an episode of* The Ronnie Barker Playhouse, *1968.*

Ronnie and friend in Hark At Barker, *1969.*

Report co-workers off in a series of their own, via his Paradine Productions company. John Cleese starred in *At Last The 1948 Show*, Ronnie Corbett appeared in *The Corbett Follies* and Ronnie Barker moved into *The Ronnie Barker Playhouse*. 'David always had that business sense,' says Ronnie C. 'Ronnie and I were quite the reverse. It was always enough for us to do the work. Basically, we didn't want to be management. But he set Ronnie up with a series and he did a series with me, written by Graham Chapman, Eric Idle and Barry Cryer, and he also did *At Last The 1948 Show* with John. So he really got us started.'

The One Ronnie

His first-time with top-billing on television, *The Ronnie Barker Playhouse*, took a leaf out of Jimmy Edwards' book and featured Ronnie in six separate one-off half-hour sitcoms, each in many ways a potential pilot for a future series. It was yet another opportunity for Ronnie to show his considerable range, playing, among others, a Welsh champion reciter of verse, an aged aristocrat, an escapologist, a bashful Scotsman and a silent monk. Two of the episodes were penned by the *Foreign Affairs* team of Mortimer and Cooke, three of them by the playwright Alun Owen, one of which – *Ah, There You Are* – finally put a name to Barker's eccentric aristo, Lord Rustless.

Ever since *A Home Of Your Own* in 1964, Ronnie had been toying with the idea of writing a similar dialogue-free film himself. The result was 1969's *Futtock's End*. 'You didn't think about it every day or every week or every month, but occasionally I thought, "I really must write one of those. I'm sure there's a lot that one can do without any words and I like complicated things."

It was a very complicated thing to write. Someone said to me it must have been very easy because you didn't have to write any dialogue. But it was the hardest thing to write because you have to lace all these things together. It was a very thick script, even though there wasn't a word spoken. I started by writing all sorts of characters and then each one had to have a line on what they were like and what they did, and then they all went off to this weekend and combined.'

The result was a very funny film – Prince Charles numbers it among his favourites – that allowed Ronnie to indulge his love of filming and gave him yet another chance to play with the character of Lord Rustless (although he is referred to as 'General Futtock' in the movie).

The movie was written in part for actor Michael Hordern, whom Ronnie knew from a TV advert that had done together for tinned soup. 'We were Mr Crosse and Mr Blackwell. That was the only time I'd met him before that. He was a lovely fellow, very funny, lovely sense of humour and loved to joke. I wrote *Futtock's End* for him and I sent the script to him saying, "I've written this for you Michael." And he said, "I can't do it Ronnie. I'm going to play Lear. I must prepare for *Lear* and I can't do any other work. But send the script, I'm sure it'll be funny to read." So he read it and rang me and said, "I've got to do this." I said, "What about *Lear*?" He said, "Well, naturally I'm doing *Lear* but I think I can study it," and in fact I've got a home video somewhere of him sitting around learning his lines for Lear where we shot it up in Stanmore at W S Gilbert's house'

The format of the almost-silent movies – or the 'grumble and grunt movies' as Ronnie refers to them – was something he would go back to years later in *The Two Ronnies*, making two further films, *The Picnic* (1975) and *By The Sea*

I have seen the future, and it's funny. All The World's A Stooge, Six Dates With Barker, *1971.*

'We said *GOODBYE* on the Friday and meanwhile Bill Cotton had been saying, "I think I can get those two fellas." He'd no idea *WE'D BEEN SACKED*'

(1982). 'I've always loved comedy where everyone in the audience knows what's happened but the actors don't. There's one scene in *Futtock's* where they're all having tea in the garden and the maid brings a plate of cakes and as she puts the tray down one of the cakes falls off and the dog picks it up and runs off with it into the woods. And then this boy grabs the cake and throws it over the wall and it lands in the water and he gets it, wrings it out and throws it again and the dog runs back, drops it, the maid sees it on the floor, picks it up and puts it back on the tray, and Rustless picks it up and puts it back on his plate. And no one knows what has happened except the audience.'

In his desire to ensure that his movie would be as good as it could be, *Futtock's End* saw Ronnie all but co-directing with Bob Kellett. 'I know I had a reputation for being very pernickety: "Oh he wants to do it again." But I knew the reason I had to do it again would be because the audience would see if you didn't do it right. They don't care about the perspective of the sound, what they care about is the person in the foreground. They used to grumble – "Oh, he's a bloody nuisance, he is." I know they did that because people have told me. But you've got to get it right.'

Sticking with Rustless (and returning him his rightful name), Ronnie spun him off into his next series, *Hark At Barker*. Running for two seasons in 1969 and 1970, *Hark At Barker* used Rustless as host for a look at a variety of topics from Females to Britain's Military and from Communications to Cooking.

From his country seat of Chrome Hall, his lordship would expound each week on the given topic, allowing for a series of sketches featuring

Ronnie in a number of roles, upwards of 50 or so per series. 'He would be speaking to the camera and he'd say, "Today, I want to talk about transport today. I mean it's absolutely a mess..." Then he'd start by saying something like, "My great uncle used to be a bus driver..." then you would cut to me playing a sketch as a bus driver, or something. The sections were quite lengthy, they weren't just links. In fact, I used to think the sketches were almost an intrusion. They almost got in the way of this daft lecture that this man was giving, although I wanted to do them at the time. But this half-hour was a visit to Chrome Hall and the person who owned the place spoke to you about his life. And I thought that the sketches may have intruded a bit.'

Sticking as always with the people he knew and could rely on, he added Josephine Tewson to the cast as Miss Bates, the secretary who was hopelessly in love with Rustless – not that his lordship ever noticed.

Among the other characters was a wizened old gardener who went by the name of Dithers. 'Ronnie had invented this character,' recalls David Jason, who was to play the wrinkled pruner, 'who I think he wanted to play – but then Ronnie wanted to play all the characters, so there you go – anyway, he was this hundred-year-old gardener. The producer Humphrey Barclay, who'd produced a series I had just done called *Do Not Adjust Your Set*, was looking for for someone and they knew they couldn't use an old person because they'd never be able to do what Ronnie would require. So Humphrey Barclay suggested to Ronnie that I should play Dithers. Ronnie and I hit it off and got on so well that I was from then on, constantly gainfully employed as long as Ronnie was.'

Having played around with Rustless for two series, Ronnie was keen to get back to the Playhouse format. The result was *Six Dates With Barker*, Ronnie's last ever series for ITV.

Once again, the show featured six unconnected tales, this time hinged on the fact that each took place at a specific point in history, ranging from 1899 with Spike Milligan's *The Phantom Raspberry Blower Of Old London Town* (later expanded into a *Two Ronnies* serial) to the year 2774 with *All The World's A Stooge*, a curious future vision of a world where humour has become a dominant religion. The latter was penned by a certain Gerald Wiley.

Former Frost alumnus John Cleese also contributed an episode, *Come In And Lie Down*, one of the few examples of Cleese's solo writing.

More importantly however, *Six Dates* served the purpose of cementing Ronnie's relationship with the man who, alongside Ronnie C, would become the best remembered working partner of his career.

Bernard McKenna's script *The Odd Job* dealt with a suicidal man who employs an itinerant to help him arrange his own death, then backs out, only to find the other guy likes to see a job finished. (It was later remade as a movie starring Python's Graham Chapman.) When it came to casting, producer Humphrey Barclay suggested using Rustless' former aged gardener, David Jason. 'Certainly from that moment when we first met, it was wonderful,' recalls Ronnie. 'We became soulmates, really. It's strange because with both David and Ronnie C, I've had such a connection. It's extraordinary. Always work with little men, you see. It really gelled with him.' 'I was away, holidaying on the south coast,' David Jason remembers landing the role in *The Odd Job*. 'I got a message to call my agent and he said, "they're doing one of the Ronnie Barker things, and he's keen to know if you want to play a character in it." They wanted to know as soon as possible so they sent the script down to me, I read it and got on the phone immediately. Yes, of course I'd love to do it. There were two super parts and I said, "I expect Ronnie wants me to play the husband, does he?" When they replied, "No, he wants you to play Clive, the loony," I couldn't believe it, and said, "that's the funniest part, the best part." When I talked to the producer later, I had to clarify that I was wanted to play the odd-job man and that surely Ronnie was playing that role. But he said, "No, Ronnie wants you to play it," which was amazing. Playing that role sealed our joint fate. Ronnie and I enjoyed working together so much."

Ronnie and David would continue working together until the former's retirement, having clearly found a rapport and performing relationship that delighted both men.

"Ronnie was a brilliant comedy character actor. There weren't many about, there were a lot of comics, but only one Ronnie Barker. There was no finer comedy actor in the country, so when he said something you listened," recalls Jason of their early work together. "I was fortunate enough to recognise his talent, because I'd been doing a lot of comedy and could see how far ahead of the game he was. So I thought that if I just watched and inwardly digested, I might learn something from him. With that kind of trust came the ability to enjoy each other's work. He knew I had instant timing, which Ronnie respected and admired. Because his timing was so specific, he needed someone who had equally good timing in order to get his material to work."

Again acting as a series of individual pilots, *Six Dates With Barker* didn't initially yield

another series. However, seventeen years later it would come good when Ronnie took Hugh Leonard's script *The Removals Person* – the tale of a short-sighted furniture removals man named Fred on Coronation Day, 1937 – and transformed it into *Clarence*, his final sitcom.

Most people who have starred in a string of successful television shows don't get sacked. But the powers that be at ITV's Associated Rediffusion weren't happy with David Frost and while they were keen to keep the two Ronnies on, Frost had them contracted to his own company. So sacked they were. It was to prove the most fortuitous of firings. 'I think David Frost was more sacked than we were,' remembers Ronnie C. 'Paradine was sacked. And then Ronnie and I were doing a sketch at the BAFTA awards live from the Palladium. I don't remember it being particularly earth-shattering, but anyway, that is the evening that Bill Cotton said, "is there any chance of getting these two for the BBC?" '

'We said goodbye on the Friday,' Ronnie B concurs, 'and meanwhile Bill Cotton had been saying, "I think I can get those two fellas." He'd no idea we'd been sacked and he thought he snatched us from the jaws of ITV by offering us a contract to do *The Two Ronnies*. So we said, "Um, we'll think about it, Bill," but we were rubbing our hands with glee. He thought he'd pinched us from ITV and in fact we'd just been sacked. Timing was everything.' ⌐⌐

Chapter FOUR

The Two Ronnies

WE were a pair, a twosome, and all we needed then was a show. They asked what we should call it and someone in the office said, "Well, they're always called two Ronnies so why not call it *The Two Ronnies*. So we did. It's the most simple title in the world.'

History already tends to view *The Two Ronnies* as a 'cosy' show. *Monty Python's Flying Circus* was in fact a contemporary and was generally seen as ground-breaking and

seasons. They were in essence removed by a generation from the Ronnies as performers. Ronnie Barker had come from straight acting and had never performed a comedy act as such in his life; Ronnie Corbett was a stand-up, but he was equally at home in London nightclubs as he was at the end of the pier.

Even more significantly, they were unique as a double act in that they weren't actually a double act. Firstly, both men worked extensively in solo projects but, more importantly, in terms of their shows together, both were comics and

'I don't think you could name a comedian now who hasn't done NEWS ITEMS. But we were the first to do them, apart from DAVID FROST'

form-bending in all manner of ways. But it's easy to forget just how innovative the Ronnies were in their day. It remains just about the only other television show that all of the *Python* team actually wrote for, indeed Cleese occasionally appeared during the first season.

There's a tendency to bracket Ronnie B and Ronnie C with that other much loved double act of British television Morecambe and Wise. But Eric and Ernie had started their television career more than a decade beforehand. Their background was one of music hall and summer

both were straight men. They could feed or they could deliver equally, always reversing the roles between them. It's impossible to imagine Ernie without Eric, but not Ronnie without Ronnie. 'We were two character men, really. It's very difficult to say what a comic is as opposed to a comedy actor or a character actor. I suppose the definition is the man who gets all the laughs is the comic. Or he works alone and feeds himself. But we didn't really fall into that category. You either called us character actors or you called us comic actors who worked much better together.

Ronnie B and Ronnie C, **The Two Ronnies;** *great character comedians (circa 1977).*

I suppose there weren't other people doing it when we started so it was to that extent unusual. But it was an acted piece.'

The format of their show was also unique for its day, drawing heavily not only on the standards of television variety but also on the work of the Frost shows. The musical numbers that became the finale of each show had begun life back on *Frost On Sunday*, courtesy of writer Dick Vosburgh. Ronnie B's monologues had also started on Frost, while their opening and closing news items were a direct lift from Frost's Continuous Developing Monologue. 'We borrowed shamelessly from David Frost's clipboard jokes, with his permission, because we were under his aegis then, because we were contracted to Paradine Productions for the first five series of *Ronnies*. The news desk was the thing. I don't think you could name a comedian now who hasn't done news items. But we were the first to do them, apart from David, who had a clipboard to announce the news in the *Frost*

Report and *Frost On Sunday*. Then we had the serial in the middle and then we had the musical thing at the end. So it was different, it wasn't just a sketch show but we got that format from the first episode. We talked a lot about how we'd do it beforehand.'

Ronnie Corbett concurs: 'We sat down and worked out between us a running order for the first show and it never altered. Because we were, in a way, so knowledgeable about ourselves, having been around so long, and experienced, we knew our limitations and our skills. With the opening news items we realised that it was a peculiar position with us that we could talk to an audience, but we couldn't talk to each other as people in front of an audience. Not like Eric and Ernie; we couldn't direct jokes at each other, only at them. "It's goodnight from me and it's goodnight from him" at the end was the biggest reference. We knew we couldn't talk to each other that way. So the news item piece meant that we were together in a slightly anaesthetised kind of way, but we were also slightly separate. Then we knew that Ronnie would not be himself but he would want to have his solo spot so he had his character man and spokesmen. And, because I had started doing it on *The Corbett Follies*, I would do my monologue piece and that would happen in the chair. And because we'd already found very good parody writers, we'd have a musical number to close the show, like a finale. And a film item in the middle because we had facilities to film and we could both act roles, and the rest of the show would be sketches. So it took on the shape of all these disparate items and the format never altered really because we knew what we could and couldn't do.'

Quick to point out their independence, in the weeks before the show debuted on the BBC, Messrs Barker and Corbett made their presence known in two one-off specials – *The Ronnie Barker Yearbook*, with special guest Ronnie Corbett, and *Ronnie Corbett In Bed*, with special guest Ronnie Barker. 'It might have been a sort of political thing to say – here is Ronnie Barker in a show; here is Ronnie Corbett in a show – now we're going to put them together. I think that's the only reason we

had been of our individuality, I still had – not a serious rocky period – but people were saying, "What will he do now on his own?" I had done six series of *Sorry* and that came to an end at the same time. So suddenly I was chopped down in mid-life in terms of quite a lot of my work. And had I not been so secure in myself it might have affected me more seriously. So it's a good thing we did do that. And it hopefully allowed Ronnie to retire whenever he wanted to, which he did, without feeling. "Christ, what will happen to little Ron?"

'We couldn't talk to each other as people in front of an audience. Not like **ERIC AND ERNIE**; we couldn't direct jokes at each other, only at them. "It's goodnight from me and it's **GOODNIGHT FROM HIM**" at the end was the biggest reference'
RONNIE CORBETT

did that.' Corbett agrees: 'Certainly I remember feeling quite strongly about that. And we said we wouldn't do chat shows together or interviews together. It was in a way prophetic because I had had my independence for too long before Ronnie B came along. I was more vaudeville than Ronnie, therefore I was guarding that bit as well. And, of course, the more he had successes with *Open All Hours* and *Porridge* the more it insulated us from being bunged together. But when Ronnie did decide to retire, as careful and protective as we

The Ronnie Barker Yearbook was scripted by Gerald Wiley, Dick Vosburgh, Eric Idle, John Cleese and Graham Chapman. Cleese also made an appearance, which is more than can be said for the first couple of months of the year. 'It's another reason why I was annoyed with Jimmy Gilbert. He was executive producer of *The Ronnie Barker Yearbook* and obviously it started with January. But he said he didn't think we needed the first two items. I said, "You can't cut them!" He said, "Oh yes you can! You can go straight into March." And so the titles read: *The Ronnie Barker Yearbook January/February/March* – and I thought, "God. That looks dreadful." January was something about skating and it consisted of very fast shots of lots of professional skaters falling over on the ice. I thought it would build. It would be funny the faster you cut it. But he wouldn't have it. And I think somebody may have whispered in his ear, that's gonna take us a fortnight to do that. But nowadays you could do it a lot quicker. Then Ronnie did *Ronnie Corbett In Bed*. Which was long before Madonna. Barry Cryer suggested a

were very lucky in persuading them to let us have that degree of control.'

With Gerald Wiley's name gracing the credits, right from the off it was clear that Ronnie B was also a power to be reckoned with behind the camera. Wiley wrote all of the show's serials, from the first – a costume drama parody titled *Hampton Wick*, through to such well-loved classics as *The Worm That Turned*, a futuristic vision of a world where all men were forced to wear dresses and Diana Dors was calling the shots – 'You had to make all the men absolutely butch. They had to look straight, they just had to wear dresses as a

'PIGGY MALONE is Fletcher really, slightly different, he gets on his HIGH HORSE occasionally, but more or less they're the SAME MAN'

good title for it – *Corbett In Orbit* – but Ronnie wouldn't have it.'

Ever since *Irma La Douce*, Ronnie has taken great care with his contracts, partly to avoid once again finding himself trapped in a long run of anything but also partly to avoid the notion of typecasting, something he had seen happen to two former colleagues – Harry H Corbett and Warren Mitchell, in *Steptoe And Son* and *Till Death Do Us Part*. 'We were contracted to David, Paradine Productions, for what I consider to be slightly too long a period – five years. But with the show, we were only contracted show by show, but we knew before we finished year one we were going to do year two. Then again, we

sort of badge, really. That was the fun of it. If they'd all been camping about it wouldn't have worked. But we did get a lot of adverse response from a small minority of feminists.'

Also revived was *The Phantom Raspberry Blower Of Old London Town*, adapted by Wiley from Spike Milligan's old script from *Six Dates With Barker*. 'I thought the younger viewers, especially the kids, would love it, so I thought that would make a serial. I added lots of bits.'

Two of the Ronnies' most successful creations featured in several of their serials over the years; the bumbling detective team of Charley Farley (Corbett) and Piggy Malone (Barker). 'It's been done since, *The Detectives*

The Worm That Turned, *with Diana Dors wearing the trousers, a brilliant* Two Ronnies *serial, 1980.*

Ronnie Barker

In character for the first **Two Ronnies** *series, 1971.*

was the same thing. I just thought of the names and the chaps. There again, Piggy Malone is Fletcher, really, slightly different, he gets on his high horse occasionally but more or less they're the same man. He's selfish and lazy and Charley Farley is more industrious and keen. I never know when someone asks where the characters come from. They're in your head or you bring them into your head. Sometimes you think about a specific person, but they just appeared.'

In the initial years, Ronnie reckoned he was writing up to 75 per cent of the show each week 'I wasn't very slow as a writer. I mean, I remember writing a *Two Ronnies* sketch we did about an amateur play, I went into my room at nine am and I came out of my room at five pm with it completely finished and that was about a 20-minute piece, but it had a lot of physical stuff in it that needed a lot of working out. So I wasn't very slow. I used to write the musical numbers we did at the end often in a day. And I might write two sketches a day. But I suppose that was when I was flowing.'

One thing Ronnie never wrote, however, was the show's trademark opening news items. 'We used to read about 200 every week to pick 20. And sometimes it was difficult picking 20, because we were very ruthless over it and if one of us wasn't sure about something, it was out. So we'd reduce the 200 to 20 and those 20 we would use and some of those would get cut. We used to get down to about 14 or 16. We never knew who'd written anything, so no favouritism went on.

'When I wrote I hardly ever altered any line. Not because I thought straight away the line was right, but I used to spend a long time thinking before I put pen to paper. I used to make little notes but by the time I'd got it down, which was in long hand, anyway, there wasn't much scratching out went on. And my wife would type them up.' 'His scripts are very precise,' says Sir Peter Hall. 'Very immaculate, very particular. And they relate to his extraordinary ability as an actor to time accurately in the way he says a line. I think the writer and the actor kind of coalesce in their precision, because although he's an anarchic comedian is some respects, as a performer he's about precision.'

sketches in a pile and sort out a balanced show and throw out what we don't want." He said, "I'm sure these shows'll be fine." I said, "No, please don't, because it will mess it up." He agreed eventually, so after that we always did a pile of things and would sort them all out at the end, make shows out of them. I think it's the only way to work because you then have the best stuff in the series that you did. There's also the timing to

'His scripts are very PRECISE. I think the WRITER and the actor kind of coalesce in their precision, because ALTHOUGH he's an ANARCHIC comedian in some respects, as a performer he's about precision'

SIR PETER HALL

No one, not even Wiley, worked as a staff writer on the *Ronnies*. All material was submitted freelance so there was no obligation to use anything just because someone was on staff. Only the best material would get through. Around a third more was filmed than was ever broadcast, with Ronnie B keeping a close eye on the editing, something that didn't always endear him to the BBC powers that be. 'I had a big row with Bill Cotton when he was head of light entertainment. He wanted to put a *Two Ronnies* show out when we'd only done three episodes out of eight. And I said, "You can't put it out, Bill, because we must do the whole eight and then we put all the

consider; you've got to get the show to a certain length and if you do three long sketches you can't have them all in. He didn't like the idea. I don't know why but the BBC seem to think that as soon as they've got something they should shove it out. They seem to think it'll go past its sell-by date but it won't. So that's what we did. It was invaluable to be able to say, "Well, that sketch didn't work as well did it? Let's throw it away." We've always had directors who've been very accommodating. They've always agreed more or less to do what we want to do. So they didn't need persuading. It was only the people further up who were saying they were maybe paying a bit more than they should be for it, as you have to buy a sketch even if it doesn't get shown. But it was a luxury.'

There was, of course, a visual aspect to *The Two Ronnies*. One was little, one was large. (Ronnie used to tell the audience before each show, 'If you've enjoyed it, please tell your friends. If not, just remember that we're Little and Large.') This was, however, one thing they never joked about. 'Ronnie C would always object to people mentioning his size except for me. I could mention it because he was so close to me and respected me. But we never did those jokes because he is the man who makes jokes about his size par excellence. It's exclusive to him and he never stops in his monologues. He was always saying things like, "I was cleaning out the budgie cage and the door slammed shut on me." I would occasionally say something and I didn't mind him saying things about me. I know I'm fat and it doesn't worry me if someone says I'm fat because I am. So I'm never insulted. If someone said, "God! That man looks like a great heap of blancmange!" I would object because it's untrue. But we were the fat one and the little one.'

Ronnie Corbett argues that this physical difference masked the similarity of the performers. 'I think we weren't as different as we looked,' he says. 'People think of the little one and the big fat one, but in fact we were quite similar in our styles. Ronnie always had more vocal skills because he'd been such an excellent character actor in repertory and he is a very good voice man. And I wasn't so much that but we're both pretty good actors, that was the basis of it. I think people see me more as a sort of variety comic doing patter and jokes. But I can also act in the same way as Jack Benny or Bob Hope can act. We could do that and in a way music hall comics in this county hadn't been that good actors before. So we were character actor-

comedians really. Basically our skills were very similar, we only looked different.'

With Ronnie B writing and helping edit the show, the balance of power between him and Ronnie C could easily have been thrown off balance had both men not taken care to ensure the success of their relationship. 'I wasn't interested in that sort of power or jealous of it,' admits Corbett. 'And also I knew I was in very safe hands. And I suppose that I'm better at delegating than Ronnie. I can do that. I never felt he was pushing himself forward or making things easier for himself because he was making things bloody hard, working late, going to editing suites at night and so forth. But I guess there were maybe people at the BBC who would say that Ronnie was a bigger cornerstone in the show than me. Yes, he took a lot more of the load and it may well have been what tired him out more in the long run than it did me.'

'We were always very careful to be equal,' concurs Ronnie B. 'And the writers had a brief. When you did a sketch, obviously one character would feed the other. But if I was being fed by Ronnie in one sketch, then I would be feeding Ronnie in another. And when I was writing the serials and some of the musical items, I was always careful to share it out. I did a monologue and he did his chair bit. It was always very much in the forefront of my mind, and the director's mind, that it should be like that. We could never have worked together that long if we hadn't got on. He just sort of trusted me in terms of the editing, and knew that I had that sort of feeling for things. Before Gerald Wiley was unmasked it was easy. But after that he tried to be very honest with the sketches. He'd say, "Well, it's very good, Ronnie, but I don't think it's as good as that sketch." And there would be no hesitation about dumping

Filming The Vikings *for* The Two Ronnies *at Lulworth Cove, 1985.*

Ronnie Barker

Ronnies B as Piggy Malone and C as Charley Farley, in **The Two Ronnies,** *early 1980s.*

anything that I'd written. Or changing anything. It was essential, really, that we got on so well and were very aware of each other professionally. That was one of the secrets of its success, I think.'

And successful *The Two Ronnies* were. The show ran for 12 series, a number of Christmas specials, two 'grumble and grunt' movies (*The Picnic* and *By The Sea*) and countless compilation shows that still regularly occupy primetime and Yuletime viewing, more than a decade after the last one was made. Some 20 million people regularly watched *The Two Ronnies*. As Ronnie Barker once tried to visualise it, that's about two hundred Wembley cup final crowds a week.

Over the years, there were many constants to

the show, both on screen and off. The Ronnies always warmed up the crowds beforehand – 'I used to say, "I've got three questions here. I'll read them out and then I'll say 'Three, two, one' and you all shout out the answer and we'll see how it goes. What are all men who mend shoes called? Three, two, one." "Cobblers!" they would all shout. Then I would say, "If a door doesn't have a bell, what have you got?" "Knockers!" they'd shout. Then I'd say, "If a farmer has sheep, cows and bullocks in his farm and the sheep and cows die, what would he have left? Three, two one." "Bullocks!" they'd all shout. And off we'd go.'

Their wives were always on hand, offering support. 'The Two Wives were always there. You

'If you've *ENJOYED IT*, please tell your friends. If not, just remember that we're *LITTLE AND LARGE*'

can hear them laughing away when no one else was. Thank God for them. They've been the backbone to both our careers and they are the best of chums. They really love to meet and we love being a foursome.'

As the years went on, they discussed playing around with the formula of the show, but it just seemed to work – news items at the top, such catchphrases as, 'And in a packed show tonight', a sketch or two together, Ronnie B's solo spot – generally a spokesman for some bizarre society here to either talk to you about the perils of pispronunciation or a man immaculately dressed in half a suit and half a frock – then another

sketch together or maybe that week's instalment of the ongoing serial, then Ronnie C's remarkable sit-down act, a shaggy dog story that was so deft at going off the point that the point simply became an adjunct. 'They were always overlong and Ronnie would cut them himself and then do them. And they were overlong when he did them and would be cut down. I never cut them because I thought it wasn't really up to me. The director cut them – consulting with Ronnie, of course. I might suggest a change, a line or two, but very rarely. And Ronnie, of course, retained in his stage act the best joke from every week. He took one joke every week and, of course, he's got an hour and a half of marvellous stuff now.'

Then, of course, there would be the musical number and a few late items of news before that now legendary sign off – 'It's goodnight from me,' 'And it's goodnight from him.' Occasionally they did impersonations – Ronnie B's Patrick Moore was always a winner, but mostly they played an array of comic characters, archetypes, even, although sometimes in private they did have specific people in mind. 'I've always done that with my characters. I've thought of someone who they're like. Although it won't show to the audience that I'm doing that. There was one sketch when we played two burglars and I played it like John Gielgud and Ronnie C played it like Noel Coward.'

One of the things that comes across strongly

was David Nobbs who sent in the pispronunciation first. And I did about four of those eventually. He said, "I don't know if I can write anymore." so I said, "Do you mind if I write one or two?" and it was the same with the spoonerisms. Dick Vosburgh first sent those in and I said, "Can I write more?" So I did and I love them. It was the same with the class sketch in *Frost Report*. I wrote three of those afterwards. I've always said that I'm a better script doctor than I am a writer. I've always thought that. When I read a script by someone else I know exactly what's wrong with it, I'm good at that, better than writing. I would rather someone say, "Right. There you are. Sort that out." I'm very confident that I can do that.'

One of the few changes in the show occurred

'RONNIE C retained the best joke from every week and of course he's got an hour and a half of MARVELLOUS stuff now'

from the shows, particularly in Ronnie B's solo spots, is his love of language. From spoonerisms to pispronunciation, it's something that typifies his work, both in *The Two Ronnies* and beyond. It's worth noting how regionally specific all his sitcom characters have been. From the East End accent of Fletch to the Welsh lilt of *The Magnificent Evans* to the Yorkshire stutter of Arkwright, each characterisation sees Barker playing not just simply with accents but with the specifics of his character's speech. Each has their own perfectly observed language. 'I love it. I always have loved using language. I think it

early on with the news items. Originally, they were read in character as po-faced news readers. But soon the two Ronnies started to laugh along, showing us the men behind the performers, indirectly endearing themselves even more to an already smitten audience. 'It was much more comfortable that way than when we started in episode one. We'd say something like, "The world's untidiest man died yesterday. He is now lying in a state." Then they'd cut to me and I'd be absolutely stone faced. And then after a while I think I started it because I couldn't help but laugh at the jokes. I considered it very

A typical Two Ronnies *monologue, 1986.*

Ronnie Barker

unprofessional to laugh on the stage out of character but this was different. They knew it was us, the two comics doing things like this. And I think I started. I laughed at something Ronnie said and I knew it would be OK, and the audience liked it. We never faked the laughs because I used to enjoy it very much.'

Among many memorable characters, the mock country duo Jehosaphat & Jones made several appearances, eventually cutting an album of their own in 1973. 'I love country and western, anyway, and it seemed to lend itself to us. We could do it easily. We did three appearances within the first five series or so and someone came along and said, "I want to do an album with these chaps." I used to love writing the lyrics, getting internal rhymes into things. I used to find it such a great delight when I got something exactly right. If you've got seven syllables, say, and you've got to convey a thought or a joke, you can spend all day and you can't get it down to less than eight syllables and you throw it down and twist it round. And eventually you get it in, and it's a great satisfaction.'

Ironically, given how popular *The Two*

'I'm a better *SCRIPT DOCTOR* than I am a writer. I've always thought that. When I read a script by someone else I know exactly *WHAT'S WRONG* with it, I'm good at that, better than writing. I would rather someone say, "Right, there you are, *SORT THAT OUT*." I'm very confident that I can do that'

Ronnies were before a live studio audience (and how key a part of their show this was), the element of the show Ronnie enjoyed most was filming on location. 'I loved the filming best because it's a wonderful medium, I think, in which to play with comedy. Now, I always think seeing the serials that they were slow. We used to wait for laughs in places and sometimes you didn't get them, so I look at them now and I think they could be faster, they weren't tight enough.' 'I knew he enjoyed the filming,' says Ronnie C, 'because he conceived it all and was in there calling the shots, helping the directors. And the

directors too were very understanding, because they learned so much really. We all did. I'm surprised in a way that he has retired so completely. I thought he might have directed a commercial or two or a short film, because I think that's what he enjoyed most.'

In their very first joint interview, a *Radio Times* cover story from the week of 8 April 1971, Ronnie B was keen to point out, 'We like working together and we like doing our own things – separately.' From the moment *The Two Ronnies* became a huge success, he was quick to make sure that would remain the case. ◯◯

Chapter FIVE

Ronnie Barker's Bottom!

NINETEEN Seventy-One saw *The Two Ronnies* topping the ratings, and the one Ronnie back with the Bard. Shakespeare came knocking again, ironically offering the same play as before, *A Midsummer Night's Dream*. This time, however, the role was Bottom and the production was for television, co-starring alongside Edward Fox, Eleanor Bron, Robert Stephens and (once again) Lynn Redgrave. The role of Titania was played by Eileen Atkins, whom Ronnie had known as an ASM at the Oxford Playhouse. 'We did that under extraordinary conditions. They only had two cameras. It was very early location work. I think it was video, that's why they only had two cameras. And it was done at night. Everything was done at night. It was the most elaborate make-up I ever had and it took me about five hours to get made up and I had a great snout stuck on and strange teeth and hair all over the place and a great brow. It took forever. And I couldn't eat for 12 hours because I was actually in the make-up for seven hours. I was drinking through a straw I remember, much to the amusement of everyone else. They were all tucking into their evening meal, I was trying to drink soup through a straw.'

The Magnificent Seven Deadly Sins was another inauspicious British comedy movie, this one a series of sketches based around said sins. It featured a strong collection of British comic talents – old acquaintances Harry H Corbett and June Whitfield, alongside Harry Secombe, Ian Carmichael, Alfie Bass and others – all of them generally misserved by weak scripting. Spike Milligan wrote and appeared in Ronnie's section, ensuring that the film was probably more fun to make than to watch. 'It obviously made Spike laugh. He kept ruining the takes by shouting out things. And I was a bit concerned because my son Larry was in it as an extra and he was only 12 so I didn't want his delicate ears to hear anything obscene. And suddenly I was doing my thing and Spike's voice came singing from the back, "I beg your pardon, I've done a pony in your rose garden." And I thought, "Oh God! Shut up! Madman, madman!" I told Larry he was going to be paid to do this. He was 12, and he stood in this queue and he thought he was going to get six shillings for the day and he got six pounds. He couldn't believe it. He said to me the other day, "You know you made me give three pound of it to my sister? I was very upset." '

Despite his almost unprecedented success on the small screen, Ronnie Barker has never really found the fame he deserved in the cinema. It seems that one of the major failures of the British film industry has been its inability to nurture home-grown television talent, as if the two mediums were diametrically opposed to each other. Indeed, it's something that persists today with the performers such as Rik Mayall. Despite universal acclaim and popularity on TV, his track record at the multiplex remains a series of dismal also-rans, while newer British comic talents such as Steve Coogan still seem destined to live out

The Two Ronnies *continued to go from strength to strength.*

their lives on the box in the corner rather than at the box office.

For Ronnie, it doesn't seem to have been a disappointment. 'I think I wasn't really concerned with simply appearing in a film. It has crossed my mind that I would like to direct a film, but then again with a lot of things I say, "Now, wait a minute. Who says you're qualified for that?" I say that to myself. That's why I haven't got in too deep in anything that I might have

people around who could do it. But no, I've never really hankered after film.'

Radio was also something that Ronnie simply hadn't had time for in recent years, due to his hectic TV commitments. He redressed that in April 1971 with a new show for the BBC, *Lines From My Grandfather's Forehead*, a free-form sketch show written in part by Barker. 'I got the name from a thing that Frank Muir once said, he said he was thinking of writing something called

'I have **HELD BACK** on a lot of things where I've thought, "No, you're **NOT RIGHT** for that." Even sort of heavy things in the theatre. I'd say, "**PEOPLE THINK** of you as a comedian. Those doors have closed behind you. You shouldn't be attempting that kind of stuff. You **CAN'T DO EVERYTHING**, so don't" '

done. I have held back on a lot of things where I've thought, "No, you're not right for that." Even sort of heavy things in the theatre. I'd say, "People think of you as a comedian. Those doors have closed behind you. You shouldn't be attempting that kind of stuff. You can't do everything, so don't." So no, I never really pursued film. And also, of course, I wasn't asked. Obviously they did the film of *Porridge* and they asked me to play the part of Fletcher. I'm glad they did because there weren't many

Leaves From My Dining Room Table. So I got *Lines From My Grandfather's Forehead*. It was just a mish-mash of stuff but it was good in that it was completely catholic in its taste. Everyone submitted things. Radio was so easy, with the script in your hand. You did the whole thing in about four hours. We had no audience for that, which made the thing a lot easier, although I prefer to have an audience. I'm always more nervous if there isn't one. But it was fun to do because you could do anything, any snippets, four lines of doggerel, could come in. 'That was the last time I did radio. Television is – dare I say it? – much more important than radio, certainly to me. I'm afraid I hardly ever listen to the radio now at all.'

Rustless Returns

1972 saw Ronnie's first foray into sitcom since *Foreign Affair*. It was an area in which he would ultimately find his greatest personal successes – and indeed his only failures. Building on the success of *The Two Ronnies*, and as always eager to pursue the solo route, he was keen to find the right vehicle, when producer and by now longtime associate Jimmy Gilbert sent him a script for a new show called *Some Mothers Do 'Ave 'Em*. 'Immediately I read it I thought, "This is not me at all. This is a knockabout, a physical comedian's part, a): I couldn't do half the things in this; and, b): I'm a lines man, I'm a dialogue chap." Thank God I did say that because Michael Crawford made such a wonderful success out of it. I was delighted I didn't do it.'

As he would so many times in his career, Ronnie came back to a character he knew. Lord Rustless – in all his guises – remains a constant in Ronnie Barker's career, so naturally he turned to his Lordship for his first starring role in a sitcom, *His Lordship Entertains*. 'I went back to Rustless because I loved him so, I loved playing him. And he hadn't been done enough. Even in the silent films he's still the same character. I just love him, the dotty old fool.'

This time, however, Barker decided to write the series himself. As with all his writing efforts, the modest actor took a pen name, this time that of Jonathan Cobbold. 'I think the challenge was part of it. It wasn't easy. You have to see the big canvas in front of you, so you're not phased if,

firstly, it takes you longer and, second, you have to find more space to expand in many directions. You've got to flesh it out. So it didn't worry me but I thought it is different. 'It's a step forward, isn't it? I've never written a full-length play. I've often thought about doing that. I've toyed with the idea of writing a stage play for Rustless. Not that I would ever play it now, but I did toy with the idea. Obviously, he'd be the squire of the village. I was going to call it *Raspberries From The Garden*, because it's a very English thing, and the curtain would go up and you'd hear (Ronnie makes a loud raspberry sound) that gets rid of the title. But I never got round to that.'

The BBC apparently wiped the tapes of *His Lordship Entertains*, denying us a chance to witness a show that would now be of interest for many reasons. '*Fawlty Towers* Mark One, I call it. It was a daft hotel, run by a man who was quite incompetent at running a hotel. I suppose the two stories so far, they are identical. Mine was a dotty old fellow and the other one was a sort of demented, opinionated man who suffered no fools.'

By now writing, which is something that Ronnie had originally begun out of necessity, was a fully-fledged second career, albeit one that was ostensibly hidden from the majority of the viewing public. It would remain a dominant side of Ronnie's career right up until his retirement, his final series, *Clarence*, being penned by one Bob Ferris. 'When I came to write situation comedy, and I didn't write many, the same sort of things from sketch writing apply. You have to have a funny situation. The situation in a sitcom has to have more possibilities because a sketch only lasts three minutes and a sitcom lasts thirty. So you have to see the possibilities before you start writing it, ask

Lord Rustless returns in His Lordship Entertains, *1972.*

Ronnie Barker

His Lordship Entertains *a chambermaid in what Ronnie calls* Fawlty Towers *Mark One, 1972.*

create a repertory company around himself. *His Lordship Entertains* was no different, featuring once again Josephine Tewson, the actress he had first spotted in *The Real Inspector Hound* and had recruited for *Frost On Sunday*. She would continue to work with Ronnie throughout his career, eventually recreating her role in *The Removals Person* episode of *Six Dates...* in Ronnie's final series, *Clarence*.

Perhaps more important, however, was the opportunity *His Lordship Entertains* gave Ronnie to develop his relationship with David Jason. When they first met, Jason still had his day job as an electrician. Working on *The Odd Job* together they both knew they were onto something special. Ronnie's first sitcom allowed them to take things further, establishing a relationship that would come to full fruition in *Open All Hours*. 'He always called me guv'nor. I was the guv'nor, meaning his main man. And when I retired and he'd done so well, with *Fools And Horses* and things, I said, "Now you're the guv'nor. I'm the ex-guv'nor. I'm going to resign the guv'norship and give it to you." And I wrote a long poem which I read out at some party we had and handed over the guv'norship to him. It was written as a sort of stand up monologue. I did that three or four times. We used to have some wonderful dinners after filming for *Open All Hours*, up in the wilds of Yorkshire. Once we

yourself where you can go in this series. But I've had so many good teachers. Muir and Norden to start with, although that was more of a sketch format in a way, they were sort of elongated sketches. But certainly Clement and La Frenais and Roy Clarke. I'd had such good teachers that by the time I'd thought that something could make a series I wasn't concerned that it wouldn't, based on my experience of the other sitcoms. You had to have good characters, you had to have idiosyncrasies about those characters and they had to have a sort of developing feel. When you watch a good sitcom you grow to like the characters and you grow to learn what they do and what their failings are and what their good points are. So that has to develop within the series.'

Throughout his career, from his days at Aylesbury onwards, Ronnie Barker has sought to were celebrating David's birthday, and David was always going on in a jocular way saying to me, "Why is it that whatever I do you come up and top it?" He's a great comedy grumbler. He used to call himself the Little Feed and I remember writing a long poem, in Shakespearean meter or something, about the Little Feed and how one day he won't be the Little Feed any more. I'm sure we were terribly good for each other. As indeed it was with Ronnie C.'

A Brief Silence

Things were going well for Ronnie Barker. His family life was secure – a loving wife, three healthy children and a spacious home in the quiet suburbs of Pinner. His career was going from strength to strength, the continued success of *The Two Ronnies* affording him just about every opportunity he wanted to pursue. Something had to go wrong. That something caught up with him the night he lost his voice while appearing in a pre-West End run of *Good Time Johnny*, a Jimmy Gilbert musical based on *The Merry Wives Of Windsor*. Set just after the First World War, Ronnie was playing the Falstaff role, the part that would later presage his retirement. 'I lost my voice. And one of the chaps who was in it said, "My brother's a doctor, an ear, nose and throat chap, you must see him." So on Sunday I went to see

him and he looked down my throat and he said to his nurse, "Oh, nurse? Come and have a look at this, this is interesting." And immediately I thought, "God, what's that?" And they saw a growth on my vocal chords and he said, "I've got to operate on that." So I had to come out of the show. The night before the operation, he said, "You've got to give up smoking," and he took my cigarettes and lighter and threw them out the window. This surgeon! Extraordinary behaviour. I remember that night, sitting in the bath in the hospital and singing all my favourite songs because I thought I may never sing them again. He said, "There's a possibility it may impair your voice. It's a very delicate operation cutting a bit off your vocal chords. I hope it won't because I know how important it is for you." '

The operation proved to be a complete success. The surgeon removed a pre-cancerous growth without any damage to Ronnie's vocal chords. A full and speedy recovery followed. By comparison, *Good Time Johnny*, metaphorically at least, died on the table.

'David always called me **GUV'NOR**. I was the guv'nor, meaning his main man. When I retired and he'd done so well, with **ONLY FOOLS AND HORSES** and things, I said, "Now you're the guv'nor" '

Seven Of One...
Half A Dozen Of The Other??

Eager to find another TV vehicle, Ronnie went back to the tried-and-tested method of the Playhouse format, embarking on a series of six potential pilots. The idea was to call the show *Six Of One*, but some high-up at the BBC decided they wanted seven shows, effectively knocking the potential follow up series – *Half A Dozen Of The Other* – firmly on the head.

With *Seven Of One*, Ronnie was looking for a new sitcom; what he found were two of the most enduring comedies in the history of British television and, in the stuttering shopkeeper Arkwright and the experienced recidivist

Fletcher, his two most popular creations.

The first episode of *Seven Of One* was called *Open All Hours*. Written by Roy Clarke, it featured the penny-pinching Yorkshire shopkeeper Arkwright, a man moved only by the sight of the buxom Nurse Gladys Emmanuel. David Jason played Arkwright's much-put-upon nephew, Granville. The second episode was titled *Prisoner And Escort*, and was written by the team of Dick Clement and Ian La Frenais, whose previous credits included the seminal 1960s hit T*he Likely Lads* and it's even better 1970s sequel, *Whatever Happened To The Likely Lads?*

Prisoner And Escort told the story of one Norman Stanley Fletcher, a prisoner being

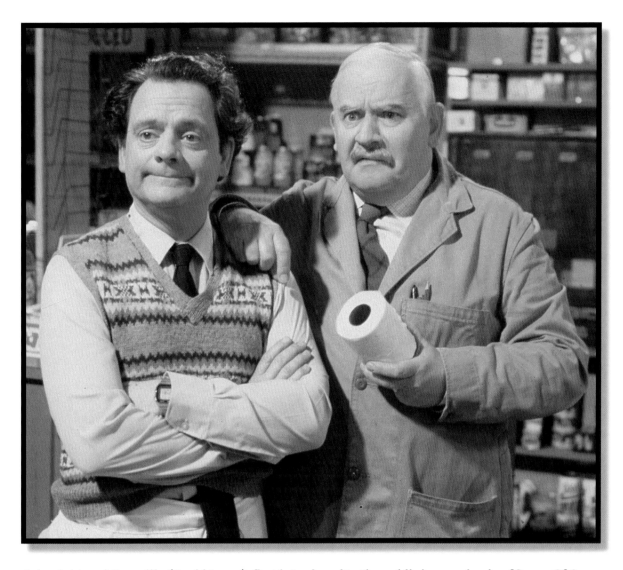

Arkwright and Granville (David Jason), first introduced to the public in an episode of Seven Of One.

escorted to his new home away from home, at her Majesty's pleasure, by two prison guards – soft touch Barrowclough (Brian Wilde) and the by-the-book Mackay (Fulton Mackay). 'We did it to find characters I wanted to play. We sat round and started thinking of characters or situations, things I wanted to do. A few years ago, in an archive file of jottings and early bits of writing, I found a piece of paper with things I wanted to do for the series and there were five of them, and the fifth one was just one word – prison. So when I met with Dick Clement and Ian La Frenais and they said they wanted to write two of these things, we had lunch and I suggested the prison idea. But I had a much more jokey perception of

it, you see. They had also thought about prison. They wanted to do one about an open prison and I wanted to do one a bit like *Bilko* in prison. So they said , "Have you got any stories?" and I said, "Well, in one of them they smuggle a woman in and she has to be dressed as a man," and I could see them going, "Umm, I don't know about that. We thought of something a bit more realistic. We'd like to do a realistic version of an open prison." But I knocked the open prison idea on the head because the thing about prison is the harshness of it. They soon agreed with that, almost immediately. So it became a security prison.'

It was an auspicious beginning; not that the

'A **FEW YEARS AGO**, in an archive file of jottings and early bits of writing, I found a **PIECE OF PAPER** with things I wanted to do for the series and there were five of them, and the fifth one was just one word – **PRISON**'

rest of the series didn't have plenty to offer as well. *My Old Man* was about a pensioner trying to save his home from the demolition crew. Roy Clarke provided another, called *Spanner's Eleven*, the tale of a down-the-league football team; and when one script proved to be below par, Ronnie himself penned *One Man's Meat*. Reunited with his former comic strip co-star from the *Today* programme Prunella Scales, Ronnie played a man forced to go on a crash diet when his wife stops him leaving the house by stealing his pants.

One of the undoubted highlights of the run was *Another Fine Mess*, written by Hugh Leonard. Ronnie and Roy Castle played two Laurel and Hardy impersonators who slowly become their characters as events escalate around them. It was an inventive idea, made memorable by two excellent performances from Castle and Barker, who both perfectly captured the detail of Stan and Ollie.

The lost gem of the series, however, was the final instalment. Written by Clement and La Frenais, *I'll Fly You For A Quid* was the everyday story of a Welsh family who will gamble on absolutely anything and everything. (The title comes from a line where Ronnie, as the dying grandfather, asks the vicar if he'll have wings in heaven. The vicar says he will. He then asks the vicar if, when he gets there, will he also have wings. Once again the vicar says yes. 'Right. I'll fly you for a quid,' the old man says and promptly dies.) 'I told the boys I wanted to play a Welsh character and they said they had got a thing about Geordies. And I said, "I can't do Geordie, can it be Welsh?" When they explained it was about a family that'll gamble on anything we decided it could be Welsh. It was a very funny piece. I played both the father and the grandfather. I'd always loved the Welsh accent and I love the Welsh sort of feeling. I think it's a good comedic noise, a good comedic accent. Although very little has been done with it.'

Ronnie was so taken with *I'll Fly You For A Quid* that when the BBC asked him which one of the seven he wanted to develop into a series, he opted for the Welsh one. While the thought of any sitcom from the team of Clement and La Frenais being lost is a sad one, Ronnie, and indeed we, should be glad.

The BBC didn't want the Welsh one; they wanted the prison one. ᴏᴏ

Norman Stanley Fletcher took his first bow in an episode of Seven Of One.

Chapter SIX

'What? With These Feet?'

PORRIDGE remains, simply, one of the best television sitcoms ever. On a par in this country with such landmarks as *Fawlty Towers* and *Dad's Army*; more than able to hold its own alongside such American classics as *M*A*S*H* and *Cheers*. Along with all these shows, it shares the hallmarks of near-perfect casting, eloquently funny scripts and excellent ensemble playing. But more than that, the one thing all these shows have in common is their ability to look beyond the laugh, to find the humour in all aspects of their character's lives – the joy, the pain, the success, the suffering. Shows of this calibre display a level of truth rarely seen in even the finest TV dramas.

Norman Stanley Fletcher had spent most of his life inside before he went down yet again for the five year stretch that lasted the three seasons (and two Christmas specials) that comprised the run of *Porridge*. He was the proverbial old lag – knew the rules, knew the ropes, looked out for young Lenny Godber (Richard Beckinsale), kept his distance from old Grouty (Peter Vaughan) and skirted round the ins and outs of the lives of a variety of other inmates.

There's an old story about *Porridge* that is still recounted by television comedy executives up and down the land. Clement and La Frenais were writing the show, they had the characters, they had the setting, they had the plot. The only thing they didn't know was what was it really about. They went to visit a recently-released inmate who set them straight – when you're inside you know you're never gonna beat the system. So you don't try. What you try and do – each and every day – is quietly win one little battle. Little victories. That's what it's all about. 'It's about little day-to-day triumphs that people need to keep their dignity, ' Dick Clement told *Radio Times* back in 1974.

Ronnie attributes a great deal of the success of *Porridge* to the realism of the world Clement and La Frenais created.'You really felt you were in a prison with maybe a bit of latitude given by those in charge to let you be a little freer and less constricted and downtrodden than you would have been in that situation. In other words, it's dramatic licence but when Mackay shouted at us you really believed he had that power over us. He was the authority figure. And Fletcher was immersed in such a realistic atmosphere and with such realistic performers. They are all what I call legit performers, straight actors, not comedy actors. Obviously with a great facility for comedy. Fulton Mackay's timing was wonderful, natural. He was very much a straight actor, very conscientious about rehearsing and never said one word different on Wednesday from what he'd said on Tuesday, which is wonderful. You never felt that Fletcher had the upper hand, that he could do exactly what he wanted with these people. That's why my character seemed real, because everyone else felt real.'

Or, as Ian La Frenais succinctly put it at the time: 'The casting – that's the key. If the actors are right, then all your troubles are over.'

'I always felt as if this was the only thing I'd ever done when I was doing it,' says Ronnie. 'I was always that person. Luckily, I've had the facility all my life for doing that. I am that person when I'm playing them, even in *The Two Ronnies* for two minutes. You don't think, "Well, in a minute I'm going to be a banged-up prisoner and here I am, sitting in a pub drinking a pint." You're only that character. Nothing else crosses your mind. You don't get outside it.'

When the commission came through to turn *Prisoner And Escort* into a series, Dick Clement and Ian La Frenais began their research by putting themselves through the admittance routine at Brixton prison. They had their medicals, handed over their clothing and possessions and spoke to many of the men they

would be writing about. 'We came out thinking, "How can we be funny about this?" ' said Clement. 'But then we thought they're surviving. Let's write about survival.'

For once, Ronnie didn't feel the need to be involved with the writing. 'You very rarely had to change anything, you just picked it up and did it. One episode I did quite a bit of writing. I think the boys weren't around and it wasn't working. But mainly it was there. We would suggest lines, of course. I remember there was one – *No Peace For The Wicked* – the one where Fletch was just trying to have a quiet afternoon and people kept coming in one after the other and Bunny Warren (Sam Kelly) came in and he was telling me a long story and I remember my foot was starting to go to sleep, so I said, "Look, Bunny, could you hurry

Fletcher did three series and one movie of Porridge, *before moving into one series of* Going Straight. *It would never be a life sentence for Ronnie.*

up, me foot's going to sleep and I'd very much like to join it, know what I mean?" I put that in and it got a good laugh. With those sort of character bits you've really got to know Fletcher. I got to know him and then suggested things that he would say and get away with. So lots of little bits like that went in. The boys were fine about it, they said this works because it is Fletcher talking.'

Ronnie did, however, initially have a hand in casting. For the role of innocent inmate Lenny Godber he suggested Paul Henry, whom he had appeared with in *Good Time Johnny*. 'Ronnie brought in Paul,' recalls producer Sydney Lotterby. 'And I had found Richard so I said, "Let's read this guy." And Richard was so good, he just convinced us. He was supposed to have a

Birmingham accent, but he quickly changed it after the first episode.' Paul Henry meanwhile kept his Brummy tones and went on to find fame as Benny in the TV soap *Crossroads*.

From day one of filming *Porridge*, the cast and crew were aware they were working on something special. 'I did the title sequence,' says Lotterby, recalling the show's austere beginning – a judge intones Fletcher's sentence over stark images of his journey to Slade prison, the doors slamming shut behind him. 'It was very different then. You couldn't normally do titles without music and the like, but we had a little bit of drama with the prison doors closing, the keys rattling in the doors. That was the first time I'd ever done a sitcom without music to open it. The writing was so good, of course, it was Dick and Ian at their best. And the performances were great. That's what made it so successful.'

A-A-A-A-A-A-Arkwright

Porridge was an instant hit with audiences but after two seasons Ronnie decided he didn't want to take the role of Fletcher any further. 'I had the awful lesson of Warren Mitchell and Harry H Corbett, you see. They stayed too long in their series. That was very instrumental in me coming out of *Porridge*. I said, "Right. I've done that, now I want to do the shopkeeper, *Open All Hours*." And I suppose I had a bit of clout so I could say to them I really want to do this. So they said, "OK. Fine. But we might come back to *Porridge*." I said, "Yes, we might," but I didn't want to get stuck. I didn't want to get trapped there, having the choice of two which I was lucky to have, I think I successfully dodged the typecasting. Maybe only just. They knew I could be different people. And *Porridge* and *Open All Hours* were so different, the characters were so different they thought, "Oh, he can do it. We can give him another series of something else, it doesn't matter." And *Two Ronnies* was going on all the time and I was doing about ten characters a week.'

'Ronnie just didn't want to be stuck in the one character,' explains Syd Lotterby, who also handled producing/directing chores on *Open All Hours*. 'He didn't want people saying, "Oh, Ronnie Barker, he's that prisoner." '

Open All Hours was not an instant success on its debut, largely, Ronnie felt, because of the decision to screen it on the less watched BBC2. 'They said, "We think it's a bit more gentle," and that's always a dangerous word because they don't think it's as funny. And on BBC2 if you got one and half million or one and three quarter million viewers – that was a vast difference. One was a success and one was a failure.'

Ronnie had other options, of course. His postcard collection had swelled to such proportions that it had turned into a cottage industry, with Ronnie releasing two collections of the cards in book form – *The Book Of Bathing Beauties* in 1974 and *The Book Of Boudoir Beauties* in 1975. Both went on to become best-sellers; several more would follow.

A series of well remembered adverts for Sekonda watches was proving highly lucrative (ironically, fellow Frost alumnus John Cleese could be seen on TV hawking Accurist watches around the same time) and a role in JB Priestley's *When We Are Married* saw Ronnie reliving his theatre days, albeit in a television production of the Shaw classic. 'It was the second play I ever did in rep and I remembered the part of the photographer so well, and I thought at the time, "One day, when I'm older, I'd love to play that." I was so pleased when I was asked to do it as it fulfilled an ambition I'd almost forgotten about. Because there wasn't an audience I felt very nervous, trembling, really. You get a little bit nervous, obviously, when you're doing a *Porridge* or an *Open All Hours* in the studio, but with this I was all over the place. I was scared of it but I knew I could do it as well as I could do it. I've never worried about that because I do it as well as I can and I can do no better. And you will certainly not do worse. So there's no point in saying, "Am I good enough for this?" Because you will find out if you're good enough if someone asks you to do it again. Or doesn't ask you.'

Ronnie as Arkwright in *Open All Hours*, 1976.

Ronnie as Friar Tuck in Richard Lester's Scottish Robin And Marian, 1976.

Turning Scottish In Spain

Movies too were once again on the cards, when Ronnie was offered the plum role of Friar Tuck in Richard Lester's *Robin And Marian*. It was a promising idea, picking up on the romance between Robin Hood (back from the Crusades after something of a delay) and Maid Marian in their later years, casting Sean Connery and Audrey Hepburn in the title roles. It was not the first time Ronnie had worked with director Dick Lester. 'I had re-dubbed Jack Shepherd as the underwater vicar in his *The Bedsitting Room,*' explains Ronnie. 'My son Adam was in *Wycliffe* with Jack for three series and told him that. Jack was rather surprised.'

Robin And Marian was shot on location in Spain during the summer of 1975. For Ronnie, it was not a happy experience. 'Awful. I'm afraid I didn't get on with Dick Lester, really. He's a very clever man but our personalities didn't mesh. I remember him saying, "You're in the foreground of this scene. Do something funny." And I said, "Well, what do you want me to do? There's nothing in the script." He said, "Just think of something." That sort of thing never pleased me at all. If you want something funny there, say it to the writers. You don't say it just before a take. I had problems with him during the dubbing, too, because he continually wanted me to say things when my mouth wasn't moving. I'd be standing there on screen and he'd want me to say something like, "Look out! Someone's coming." And I'd explain, "But my lips don't move, Dick." "No one'll notice," he'd say. "Well, I will. That's half of my performance, what I say." So he got annoyed with me and in the end he got someone else in to impersonate my voice. Guess who he got? David Jason. I listen to it now and I hear David. He did several people in the film, all saying

'I had the *AWFUL LESSON* of Warren Mitchell and Harry H Corbett, you see. That was very *INSTRUMENTAL* in me coming out of Porridge. I said "Right. I've done that, now I want to do the shopkeeper, *OPEN ALL HOURS*"'

things when their mouths don't open. So me and Dick parted not on the best of terms, really.'

Ronnie's relationship with his fellow actors was more convivial when the situation allowed, on what was obviously what movie publicists term a 'troubled shoot'. 'I often had Nicol Williamson and Denholm Elliott at each other's throats. I was sort of keeping them apart. I was in the middle for the whole ten weeks, really.' Robert Shaw, who had recently finished filming *Jaws* and was cast here as the Sheriff of Nottingham, proved equally mercurial. 'I remember we were having a half day and it was lunch. And everyone had had a few, I think, and Robert Shaw was saying how he loved playing boules. Now I've played it a bit. And he was always challenging people to things to show he was best. So he said to me, "I'll bet you a hundred pounds, I'll give you eight points and I'll beat you to 13 points." I said, "OK." Everyone came out to watch us, it was like a tournament. And he started to catch me up. We got to the point where he had a ball right next to the jack and – they were all rooting for me in a way, the other actors – I had one ball left and I thought I had to bomb him out

of there. I have to do this. So I took aim and it flew right out and a great cheer went up. He was very angry, very upset about it. He went, "Bastard!" and threw his money down. But I felt so elated. It was like David and Goliath really, the feeling of it. He was a nice man, but he was aggressive.'

Tensions on the set of *Robin And Marian* moved into the realm of the surreal when Dick Lester, having realised that Sean Connery was playing Robin with his customary Scottish brogue, decided that the rest of the merry men should lose their north-country accents and play the whole thing Scottish. This was, after all, only half-way into production.

Grumble And Grunt

For a self confessed 'lines man', Ronnie Barker has shown a continued passion for the almost silent film. Between set-ups on *Robin And Marian*, he wrote another. *The Picnic* featured a similar ensemble to the country aristos of *Futtock's End*. Lord Rustless – though never mentioned by name – was back and Ronnie Corbett was along for the first time. 'They were, I suppose, a challenge. It was much more exciting to me than either of the

'DICK LESTER got annoyed with me and in the end he got someone else in to impersonate my voice. Guess who he got? DAVID JASON'

other two because I wanted it to capture that sort of far-off childhood summer. The sort of feeling you remember of slight weirdness. Although everything was funny in it, there was still a feeling of an unreal little encapsulated world. Which is the same with the others to a degree. In *The Picnic* you have an Edwardian sort of picture. It's a situation that is unreal to most people, and that's what I liked about it. And this man who just sort of rode over everyone and behaved how he wanted to and everyone else just sort of fitted in. I loved that kind of thing hugely.'

Broadcast on New Year's Day, 1976, *The Picnic* was a highlight of *The Two Ronnies'* career, a delightful collection of sight gags and comic moments, imbued with the Ronnies' usual level of sauce and double entendre. 'We used double entendre all the time. Not much single entendre went on. Occasionally I'd find myself holding myself back over some things. I'd say to Ronnie, "Oh we can't say that." So there was censorship going on between us, within the programme. You'd never leave an unfinished rhyme that started out with something like "duck", you would never do that. I remember we did a harvest festival thing, with jokes like, "he sits amongst the cabbages and peas." And that's an ancient one, but we had to change it to, "He sits amongst the cabbages and leeks." ' *The Picnic* proved so popular that the Ronnies

returned to the format in 1982 with *By The Sea*.

Both films were clearly influenced by the postcard humour that had become Ronnie B's other passion and in many ways it's easy to see *By The Sea* as a culmination of all that, itself something of a sentimental postcard to the seaside humour of bygone days. 'It is, absolutely. It's sort of a harder film than *The Picnic* and *Futtock's End* – which is very moody. But this was a harder, glossier version of both of those earlier ones. *By The Sea* was much longer, it originally ran an hour and 25 I think. There again I crossed swords with Jimmy Gilbert. He cut it to 55 and I said, "It's just about OK, I suppose." Then he said, "I think I'm gonna cut it to 35." And I said, "Well, if you do I'm out of here. That's murder, Jimmy. That's not cutting, that's murdering it." He left it at 55.' To emphasise its origins, the BBC produced a book of comic postcards to publicise the one-off special. 'It was fun to do because of that humour. We had the beach huts and those things you put your head through. They're all out-of-date things. The girls were dressed in a very modern way, but it was of days gone by. It wasn't modern. It could've been any date. It was 1930s in feel.'

Among the compromises Ronnie felt he made with *By The Sea* was the movie's final gag, which involved a small dog which had been annoying

Vending over backwards, Ronnie in the rarely seen **Spanner's Eleven, Seven of One,** *1973.*

***Ronnie on the eve of being released from* Porridge *so he could enjoy* Going Straight.**

everyone throughout the day and was accidentally left tied to the back of the car as it drove off. 'It was obviously a toy dog – the car went round the corner and it swung right out. And then they stopped the car and the dog was perfectly alright. The producer said we couldn't put that shot in, but I've seen it many times in films. I was very annoyed about that because it was the last gag of the film, but he wouldn't let me. That's what producers are there for, I suppose. To put a spanner in your work.'

Banged Up Again

Following the mild success of the little-seen *Open All Hours*, Ronnie was lured back to a third and final series of *Porridge*. The writing retained its high quality and despite an 18-month gap the cast was as fresh as ever.

Ronnie was all set to say goodbye to Fletcher

when an interesting opportunity arose. Fletch's five-year stretch was almost up – how would he cope being back in the real world?

The resulting series, *Going Straight* (complete with theme tune sung by one R Barker) was once again penned by Clement and La Frenais and also featured Richard Beckinsale, as Fletch returns home to find that Godber has moved in with his daughter Ingrid (Patricia Brake). The opening episode, *Going Home*, mirrored the pilot *Prisoner And Escort*, with Fletcher spending his return train journey to London with a departing Mackay. After that, it was life in the real world five years on.

There's always a risk changing any successful formula and while *Going Straight* was undoubtedly a strong show, something was still missing. Fletcher simply worked best when he had something tangible to react against. Put him

'We used **DOUBLE ENTENDRE** all the time. Not much single entendre went on. Occasionally I'd find myself holding myself back over some things. I'd say to Ronnie, "Oh **WE CAN'T SAY THAT**." So there was censorship going on between us within the programme'

in a small cell with an authority figure on every closely-guarded landing and he knew what to do. Put him back in the real world and everything simply became a lot more nebulous.

According to producer Sydney Lotterby, *Going Straight* was born, in part, of Ronnie's desire to once again move on. 'Ronnie didn't want to do any more *Porridge*. But he wanted to extend it. But sadly that didn't work, probably because – despite it being the same characters – the public appreciation just wasn't quite the same. They wanted to see Ronnie in prison. It got a BAFTA, but after *Porridge* it was always second best.'

'Most people said it didn't work,' agrees Ronnie. 'I don't know why. I mean, it had Godber in it, that was perfectly legitimate because she had met him in prison and it just put Fletch in different situations. But it didn't seem to go well

with the high-ups in the Beeb. It is influenced a lot, not just by the public but by the people who decide upstairs. I don't know *who* decided but they did. I get a lot of letters asking what happened to *Going Straight*. Sydney Lotterby wrote to someone very high up: "I've often wondered why you don't bring back *Going Straight*," he said and he explained all the plus points – the characters, opening up the situation, it was just as funny, got just as many laughs – "Why don't you bring it back?" Signed, "Sydney Lotterby." He got a letter back saying, "Dear Mr Lotterby, thanks for your letter. It was interesting. It's always interesting to hear from a member of the public." ' Norman Stanley Fletcher made just one more appearance, this time on the big screen in what was to be Ronnie Barker's only starring role in a movie.

The British film industry in the 1970s

'The **PUBLIC** appreciation just wasn't
quite the same, they wanted to see
Ronnie **IN PRISON**. It got a **BAFTA**,
but after Porridge it was second best'

SYDNEY LOTTERBY on GOING STRAIGHT

consisted largely of increasingly dodgy Hammer horrors in the early part of the decade and TV sitcom spin-offs for the rest. The casts of *Dad's Army*, *Are You Being Served?*, *The Likely Lads* and *On The Buses* all made appearances down the local Odeon, most of them infinitely inferior to their televisual incarnation.

Porridge was an exception. It wasn't as good as the series – again, something seems lost in the translation – but it wasn't that far off the mark. Unlike the series, the production was largely shot on location, spending eight weeks in Chelmsford prison. 'I remember we were doing something involving cigarettes and matches and one of the extras said, "They don't do that. They roll 'em thinner than that." And I thought, "Aha! He's been inside. And one or two of the extras came up and said, "No, you're doing that wrong." I remember when we were filming the movie, we were shooting a scene near a garden and there was a little chap working away there. I was standing there waiting and I asked him, "Are you in for a long time?" "Thirty years," he said. "I killed my wife." And he was this little innocent-looking man, talking about when he put his wallflowers in. I did go round and meet some of the inmates and what I remember most is the deadness of the eyes, that look of submission, almost as if they were on some kind of tranquilisers. They weren't, of course, but they had that look as if someone's really on downers. The whole experience was real. Doing *Porridge*, it felt as if it had a reality which *Open All Hours* certainly didn't have.'

A recent fire in the prison led to a few problems during filming. 'There was someone constantly drilling. You couldn't shoot. So every time they wanted to do a take they had to give this guy a fiver. He made about £400 a day.'

Several weeks after the movie finished filming, Ronnie received a phone call from Sydney Lotterby, producer/director of the TV version of *Porridge*, informing him that his co-star Richard Beckinsale had died, at the age of 31, after a heart attack. 'Richard was such a charming man and we were so close. It was a terrible shock when Syd rang me up and said that he'd died. He was in tears and I was streaming with tears. It was a terrible blow.' ᴏᴏ

Perfect on-screen (and off) chemistry. Godber (Richard Beckinsale), Fletch (Ronnie Barker) and Mr Mackay (Fulton Mackay) in the third and final series of Porridge.

Chapter SEVEN

The Two Ronnies – Live At Her Majesty's

SHE said, "What are you doing now?" And I said, "We're at the Palladium, Your Majesty – you ought to come and see us." She said, "I very well might." But she didn't.' In February, 1978, Ronnies Barker and Corbett travelled to Buckingham Palace to receive their Order of the British Empire medals. In a break with protocol, the two Ronnies were presented to the Queen together, receiving her personal thanks for all the entertainment they had provided.

Palladium,' Ronnie has said, although before they trod the boards in London they tested the show at the Hippodrome in Bristol. 'I probably initially enjoyed it more than Ronnie because I was not so nervous,' Ronnie Corbett remembers. 'But Ronnie always said he never heard a noise like it. When we came on stage with the biggest show at the time, he'll never forget the noise of welcome when the doors opened and we stepped out.'

Terry Hughes, the director of the TV show, was overseeing the production and Gerald Wiley was its head writer. The set featured a large

> **'I'm VERY PROUD to say that I'm the only person who's ever STARTED their variety career by topping the bill at the London PALLADIUM'**

That entertainment was now about to be presented to the public live for the very first time. The West End impresario Harold Fielding had for years been trying to persuade them to take their act on to the stage. Maybe it was the timing, maybe it was the money, but 1978 was certainly the year. 'I'm very proud to say that I'm the only person who's ever started their variety career by topping the bill at the London

staircase, at the top of which were two doors, one large, one small. Needless to say, Ronnie C made his entrance through the large door and Ronnie B through the small. The show closely followed the structure of the TV series – news items to begin, the usual solo spots, a musical number, plus a selection of other variety acts in support. 'I was the most nervous I've ever been. No retakes there. You couldn't stop and do that

The Royal favourite. With the Queen Mum, Royal Variety Performance, 1986.

bit again. We had some very complicated stuff, like this piece I wrote as an old Chelsea pensioner talking about all the girls he ever knew. He starts a little dance as he sings and eventually he's kicking his legs up and then he collapses. It was called Phyllis Hooter's Ball and it was all girl's names rhymed very quickly: "Clarissa you could kiss her and you could meddle with Melissa and Vanessa you could press her and caress against the wall and you could have fun with Nicola but if you tried to tickle her you'd end up with Virginia and she won't do at all..." '

The opening of the show gave Ronnie his biggest worries, however. As a performer, Ronnie has always immersed himself in his characters. Starting with the make-up, building through the costume to the point where the man on stage was completely the character, never the actor. But the opening of the show required Ronnie Barker to stand on stage as Ronnie

Barker, a prospect he did not relish, until Ronnie C made a suggestion – play 'Ronnie Barker' as a character. 'I developed a sort of pseudo-me character. Rather like in the news items, but it had to be different. So I developed a smoother delivery, a more chummy, friendly thing, which seemed to work. Ronnie thought it worked because he knew I was scared of being myself all through it. He was always himself on his chair, or the character that you think is him. So he knew I was worried about being myself. He said, "That's good. It's very avuncular, it's very smooth, it looks good. The costume's good and you look comfortable and affluent and all the things you're supposed to look in front of an audience." So I got used to it and enjoyed it eventually, although I'm talking about four weeks after we opened.'

'Once he found a way of doing it,' Ronnie C concurs, 'like an actor, it remained the same more or less each night. I would see him

Ronnie Corbett mid-monologue, the longest-shaggy dog stories ever told on stage.

remembering to put his hand in his pocket at a certain time and so on, doing the performance, because he had to have it all in his mind, I suppose. On his own admission, he can't go and open a fête or something because he doesn't know who to be.'

After all his experience performing, it might have come as a surprise to Ronnie to find that he was still capable of being nervous. 'No, it didn't surprise me, because I was nervous for *Porridge* and *Open All Hours*. Before *Porridge* I always used to lie down for half an hour with the light off, just lie there and get my brain going. That's about as much Stanislavsky as I ever did. Some people prepare for ages for a part, but I think that's suspect sometimes. Either they're not as good as they should be and they have to try very hard or they're just deluding themselves into thinking they are researching something. Some people will say, "Oh, I'm doing a country part so I have to go and live in the country for three

weeks." I always tend to suspect that a bit. I think many actors pretend that things are a lot more difficult than they are because it makes them look clever. I've worked with actors like that but I've never had it. If someone says, "You say, 'Gotcha!' and then you go over there," I say "Gotcha!" and go over there.'

The critical response to the show was mixed, with some emphasising how closely the whole theatrical event resembled a television show. 'We were slightly worried that there was hardly any new material but people assured us that audiences wanted to see us in the flesh, on stage and to see the things they knew. It was very similar to the show, really.'

Classic sketches were revived, Jehosaphat and Jones got to sing, even Fletcher got a look in, in a short sketch written specially for the show by Clement and La Frenais. Ronnie C did some of his stand-up act to equal things out. Whatever the critics had to say, the public voted with their

(Above) The Two Ronnies *take to the stage, 1977.*

money and the run was extended from its initial seven-and-a-half week run to a full three months, with the duo performing seven days a week to keep up with demand.

They then took the show to Coventry over the Christmas period in preparation for a 14-week run in Australia in May 1979. Ronnie commuted to the performances in Coventry, using his time on the train to work on another of his books, *Gentleman's Relish*. His various collections of saucy postcards and long-forgotten magazine illustrations had proved to be a rather successful sideline for the actor. 'When I published my first one, the publisher said, "This will go extremely well. Your next book will go almost as well. And the book after that will go fairly well and the book after that will be sort of alright." He said, "I can say this from previous experience. It always happens. This sort of book starts off at its peak and goes down, gradually." And he was right – the last one I did only sold about 20,000 and the first one I did sold 140,000.'

The two Ronnies and their families decamped to Australia in April 1979. They returned the following April, having remained out of the country for the full year for tax purposes. 'We worked our brains out the year before, prostituting ourselves all over the place, doing commercials and stuff, and we made a lot of money and we knew we would not be taxed at all. That was the basis of my retirement fund.' Their sell-out tour was confined to eight weeks in Sydney and six in Melbourne. For the rest of the year, Ronnie C did occasional concerts and stand-up work, while Ronnie B sat by the pool. One of the advantages of the year away was the manner in which it helped cement the friendship between the two Rons. Although they had worked closely together for many years, the two men rarely socialised, largely because of their differences in location. While both lived in London, Ronnie B was in the north west (Pinner) and Ronnie C in the south east (Croydon). 'So we went to each other's houses maybe twice a year.

The two Rons do Kid Creole and Boy George, 1983.

When you're smiling... The Two Ronnies, *circa 1978*.

*Arkwright and Granville (with hairpiece) re-***Open All Hours,** *1981.*

But now we were living in each other's pockets. He was about a third of a mile away. We both had lovely places overlooking the Harbour Bridge and it was super. The friendship really developed. Our wives went to keep fit and aerobics together and we met a lot, and, yes, we did become much closer socially. Of course, he and I were close, but as a foursome we really cemented it all in Oz. It was a lovely time.'

Re-Open All Hours

In the absence of any new material from either of the Ronnies, the BBC had decided to dust down the 1976 series of *Open All Hours* and try it out on BBC1. The result was another instant ratings success, proving Ronnie's point that the Beeb had misjudged the show's original time slot. Plans were rapidly made for a new series on Ronnie's return, five years after the original had aired.

Writer Roy Clarke revived his crusty old shopkeeper, while producer/director Sydney Lotterby reassembled the team of David Jason as Granville and Lynda Barron as Nurse Gladys

Emmanuel. Ronnie Barker meanwhile dusted down his Glenn Melvyn-inspired stutter. 'Arkwright was in the writing. Roy Clarke made him this mean, money-grabbing man and all I added was to ask if he could make him a man who stutters. He left me to put the stutters where I wanted, except occasionally he'd write a gag about it. But I used the stutter as a timing device, it was wonderful. We used to have a house in Littlehampton and there was a man 'round the corner who ran the local stores. Somebody wrote to me once and said, "Because you based your character Arkwright on this man, can you please come and re-open our new premises?" And I had to write back and say, "I'm afraid I didn't base it on him, it was based by Roy Clarke on his father, who I think had one of these sort of shops." '

Despite the five-year lay-off, Arkwright still fitted Ronnie as comfortably as, well, an old brown shop coat. 'It was easy to go back. Although David shows how much older he had gotten. He had to wear a hairpiece when we

'David shows **HOW MUCH OLDER** he got. He had to wear a hairpiece when we came back because he'd **LOST HIS HAIR** in the back. When we started he looked like a child'

came back because he'd lost his hair in the back. When we started he looked like a child.'

'Time was marching on,' agrees Jason, 'and I was having to dye my hair to try and keep around the age we thought my character, Granville, might be – which was thirty-ish. But as time moved on, it was becoming more and more difficult to try and maintain that innocence without looking like someone who isn't playing with a full deck. Granville wasn't simple, he was just overpowered by his uncle and couldn't break away from the situation. But he wasn't there because there was anything wrong with him mentally. It was just Granville.'

'It's the thing I enjoyed doing most,' recalls Ronnie. 'I think *Porridge* was the best thing I ever did, certainly, in many ways. It's a close run thing between those two, but I think *Porridge* was most successful in terms of the public's appreciation. But I enjoyed *Open All Hours* more because of David. We had such a good time

doing it and it shows, I think. You can see it on the screen.'

'I remember once, when we were doing *Open All Hours*,' says Jason, 'we did something particularly silly in a rehearsal room and really fell about laughing. Ronnie just stood there and said, "It's amazing, isn't it?" I said, "What do you mean?" He said, "It's bloody marvellous, here we are getting paid very well for making each other laugh. Not a bad life, is it?"

'I've always said that working with Ronnie, particularly on the last couple of series, was like playing top tennis,' continues the actor. 'When you see people playing tennis, it's just tennis. But when you see two top players, serving things that you think the other guy can't get, and he does, and returns it..., I've always likened that to Ronnie and I. There would be moments when I would do something unexpected and it would work – likewise with Ronnie – so we'd play games to see who could top each other. I'd invent a piece of

As Arkwright with Kathy Staff (who also played Nora Batty in **Last Of The Summer Wine***), 1983.*

business or a line, and blow me, five minutes later when we did the scene again, he's invented something even funnier than I'd done. After one or two of those you give up and say"alright, you win." ' Syd Lotterby agrees: 'I think the strength of their performances came first of all from the admiration David had for Ronnie. David used to think, "This is the man I can learn from," and he did.'

Indeed, it is a testament to Jason's respect for Ronnie that he remained playing what was essentially the second lead in a series, when he was finding full-blown stardom on his own in John Sullivan's *Only Fools And Horses*. On retiring, Ronnie handed the 'Guv'norship' over to Jason, who in many ways over the subsequent decade, through such varied successes as *Only Fools...*, *The Darling Buds Of May* and *A Touch Of Frost*, filled the gap left by Ronnie's retirement. He has certainly matched his mentor in popularity with the public. 'I suppose in a way

maybe that is true,' considers Jason. 'I'd like it to be true because in a way, I'm sort of Ronnie's protégé, really. I served my apprenticeship with him, I learned a tremendous amount from him and I'm still carrying the flag'.

Open All Hours ran for three series in the 1980s, with Ronnie once again opting to say goodbye to Arkwright at the height of his success, with a regular audience in the region of 20 million. It is a perfect example of Ronnie's perfectionism that his only disappointment with the show appears to be Arkwright's voiceovers, which closed each episode, as the shopkeeper packed away his wares, reflecting on his day. 'I never felt it worked, really. It was the one thing I didn't like much, mainly because it didn't sound like Arkwright. It was a director's thing. It was very quiet, he was ruminating. It suddenly felt strange after they'd been shouting all day in the shop. I didn't think it quite worked. I think we just didn't do it right. My fault, really. I remember

Ronnie Barker in **Magnificent Evans,** *1984.*

hardware shop in Middlesex. This man said, "We love your show and we always think there should be a sketch about our shop because," he said, "someone came in the other day and asked for four candles and I gave them these four candles and they said, 'No, fork handles.' " And I said that's a good idea. So I wrote it and then we weren't sure when we read it. The director, Terry Hughes, who's very good, said, "It's clever but I don't know if it's going to work." And then we decided to try it and, of course, we were delighted at its reception. It got twice as good during the Palladium shows because so much more went into it as we went on. Just little bits, but you knew you could relax into it.'

This was one of the few examples where Ronnie used an item sent in by the public. On another occasion, it was a photograph. 'What we did use in *Open All Hours*, somebody sent me a photograph and she said, "My grandfather used to have a shop like yours." She sent me a copy of this photo and it was absolutely me. It looked like my grandfather, who was a plumber, a whitesmith as they were called in those days. He used to wear the flat cap and the big moustache and there was this man standing outside this shop looking just like him. Then I said to Syd, "We must use this somewhere," so we had it hanging in the kitchen and I remember I wrote a few lines about it so they could cut to it and it looked so authentic.'

The Not So Magnificent Evans

By 1984, Ronnie Barker knew very little about failure. A regular fixture in the top ten TV ratings in not one but three series, it was almost impossible to imagine something he touched not turning to comedy gold. The BBC certainly thought so, priming him as one of their heavy

in the second series thinking, "I mustn't drop this into my boots, I mustn't mumble this." But even so, it's just the change in atmosphere, I think. I think it could've been much better done.'

As always, Ronnie C (who by now was starring in his own successful sitcom, *Sorry*) was gracious and grateful for his colleague's success. 'He was very good about it. He was always most encouraging about how well they were going. He was very generous, because it must be difficult if you're an equal in a show but then your partner has something that is doing very well and people are talking about it. But you never felt there was any envy or anything going on. He was very generous.'

The Two Ronnies was, of course, as popular as ever, with a 1983 return to the West End breaking all their previous records there. Among the many highlights this time round was the classic Four Candles/Fork Handles sketch, written by Ronnie, although inspired by a member of the public. 'It's the one that everyone talks about. The idea for that was sent to me by a

How? One of The Two Ronnies' *regular song routines full of double (never, ever single) entendres.*

Looking back, you can see the influence that The Two Ronnies *had on successive comedians.*

hitters in the all-important autumn schedule. *The Magnificent Evans* proved them wrong.

It seemed like a guaranteed winner – Ronnie and Roy Clarke together again. With this tale of a small-town, determinedly individual photographer and his live-in girlfriend who insisted to all and sundry that she had her 'own apartment', surely lightning would strike twice?

From Ronnie's point of view, the pattern was familiar. Just as he had first played Arkwright at the height of Fletcher's fame, so here he was offering up one Plantagenet Evans, possibly intended to take up the reigns when Arkwright was no more. It would be another example of how well the man avoided typecasting, always kept moving, always one step ahead but never failing to bring the audience along with him. Until now. As before, the producer/director was Sydney Lotterby. 'It didn't work,' Lotterby recalls. 'I think the character was perhaps a little bit too exaggerated. It was a bit like the thing that Ronnie did next, *Clarence*. The truth of *Open*

All Hours and the character, and of Fletcher, wasn't actually the same as Evans. He was too exaggerated. And to be honest, I don't think it was written as well as it could've been. Roy Clarke's a very fine writer but it just didn't seem to fit Ronnie.'

The Welsh setting of *The Magnificent Evans* had, of course, begun life in Clement and La Frenais' *I'll Fly You For A Quid*. As far back as 1973, Ronnie had wanted to do a series based around Welsh characters. Now he was getting his wish, albeit in different form. 'I had said to Roy Clarke I would like to do a Welsh character and he went away and thought about it. He came up with the idea of the photographer and the big car and all the character stuff. I enjoyed doing it but the audience didn't like it. I don't know if he was too soft a character. Sometimes he was ruminative. There was a bit of whimsy about it. But the audience preferred the harder stuff, the sharper stuff. He was a terribly rude man, very chauvinist. But he was lovely to play, swanning

'*Maybe people just thought, "We don't believe this chap."* **I HOPE IT WASN'T** *that because I would try to be as different as I could be in everything I did …and this was as* **DIFFERENT AS ANYTHING** *I'd done.*'

about in a large cape and hat. It was lovely to do and I was sad that it didn't catch on. Maybe it was just too slow, especially in the filming. We did fall in love with the scenery a bit too much and allowed it to drift us into a slow, ambling sort of pace. It was just too pretty and that made it slow. I must have been just as much to blame I suppose, although I blame Sydney Lotterby for that, really, for leaving in too much stuff. Nevertheless, when he was setting up the shots, I used to say, "Can we get that river in the background there?" So I was just as guilty as he was. Except he left it all where I would have probably said it had to go. Or maybe people just thought, "We don't believe this chap." I hope it wasn't that, because I always thought that *Porridge* and *Open All Hours* were very different characters. I've never been an actor who looks the same. Some actors always look the same, some just prefer not to use make up. But I would try to be as different as I could be in everything. And this was as different as anything I'd done.'

The failure of *The Magnificent Evans* was certainly a disappointment to Ronnie but, putting things in context, his continued popularity in *The Two Ronnies* and *Open All Hours* meant that such a flop had little detrimental effect on his career. 'It certainly didn't phase me and it didn't happen really until after we'd shot it. So we weren't there on location at eight o'clock in the morning going, "What are we doing this for anyway? People hate it." And they didn't hate it. But it wasn't as good as the others.'

In other people's eyes however, Ronnie Barker backing a loser came as something of a surprise. He had even bigger surprises in store. ◯◯

Chapter EIGHT

And It's Goodbye From Him...

AS OF January 1, I am retiring from public and professional life so I am unable to undertake any more commitments. To those people with whom I have worked, I would like to express my gratitude and good wishes. So it's a big thank you from me and it's goodbye from him. Goodbye.'

If you happened to call the offices of Dean Miller Associates on or around New Year's Eve, 1987, that was the message you would have unexpectedly heard. So who were Dean Miller Associates? 'They' were another phone line in

Wives, *Tartuffe*, *The Misanthrope* – he would've been wonderful in any of those. And during my fifteen years at the National I'd kept on asking him, offering him all these roles. But it never worked out because of the scheduling. I do think he's the great actor that we lost. I really do think that.'

'Peter Hall triggered it off but he wasn't the reason I retired,' Ronnie explains. 'The reason I retired was that the material was getting less good. It wasn't even a block. I'd run out of ideas. I was dry of ideas for sketches. Other writers had moved on and we only had David Renwick left,

'I do think he's THE GREAT ACTOR

that we lost. I really do think that.'

SIR PETER HALL

Ronnie Barker's Cotswolds home, itself named Dean Mill. The line served as Ronnie's agent for the last few years of his career, with Joy replying to the messages, generally with a 'No,' given Ronnie's ongoing commitments.

Ronnie had made the decision to retire in late 1985, shortly after Peter Hall asked him to play Falstaff. 'He should have played all the great Shakespeare comic parts,' says Hall today. 'He would've been a wonderful Falstaff, a wonderful Toby Belch, there's about fifteen parts in Shakespeare he could've done. And the Moliére parts that Moliére wrote for himself – *School For*

really. He was the only established writer. Plus, I'd done everything I wanted to do. I had no ambition left.'

'I think we felt the loss of his quality,' says Ronnie C. 'But I don't think he felt guilty over the fact that he couldn't come up with as much material as in the past. The fear he always had, and indeed I always had, was that eternal one that on Monday you read material that is all rubbish and you've got to do it on Friday.'

The announcement came unexpectedly. Just days before, *The Two Ronnies* had once again dominated the TV ratings with their now

'So it's Goodnight from me'... 'and it's Goodnight from him. Goodnight'.

traditional Christmas special. A new series, *Clarence*, was due to start a few days later. Naturally, the press speculated, ill-health being the first choice. 'I'd had a worry about the heart when I'd been on holiday in 1985. A doctor said, "I think you've had a minor heart attack." I didn't recall it. I'd just felt rotten for one evening and had to lie down because I'd felt strange. And next morning I felt alright, but this doctor said, "I think you have." Even that had no influence on me retiring at all. Nothing to do with it. They gave me tests and they put me on some blood pressure pills and that was fine.'

Others speculated – again without foundation – that the relatively recent deaths of British comic legends Eric Morecambe and

'The reason I RETIRED was that the material was getting less good. It wasn't even a block. I'd RUN OUT OF IDEAS. And I'd done everything I wanted to do, I had no ambition left'

The Barker boys Adam (left) and Laurence (right), celebrate an evening of paternal triumph at the British Comedy Awards, 1990.

Tommy Cooper played a part in this decision.'None at all. It's never worried me. You've got to die. It's very sad, awful. I hated the fact that we'd lost Eric and Tommy Cooper. And Les Dawson was a wonderful performer as well. I didn't know him, but Eric I got to know in the last four or five years of his life and he was a very funny man. Off stage he was continually funny. He came to our house in Pinner once for dinner. He was very shy. He didn't like eating out so he used to be a bit reticent about going anywhere. But he said he would come and he did. A car brought him and his wife and I went to the door and the driver was there and Eric said, "Hello, Ronnie. How are you?" Then he looked past me, looked around the hall and said back to his driver, "About an hour." He was a wonderfully funny man.'

As Ronnie put it, the well had simply run dry.

He had nothing left he wanted to do, no more ambitions to achieve. (Well, maybe one, but more of that later). 'The situation sort of pushed me, goaded me into asking, "Well, haven't you done enough?" And I had. Peter Hall's thing showed me I shouldn't be doing this anymore. "You are much happier not doing it, you are much happier being in the Cotswolds." If I hadn't said it, in about a year and a half somebody high up in the BBC would've said, "We've had enough of these two." I'm sure they would and I didn't want that. Quit while your ahead, that was my slogan.'

The Two Ronnies' first series in Australia was to be their final series. After a career spent at the BBC, their last run was on Kerry Packer's Channel 9. The show was similar to its English cousin, comprised of sketches from the two most recent UK seasons. The news items were

Still smiling, still friends, still **The Two Ronnies** *at heart.*

dropped, as was the serial, but Jehosaphat and Jones became something of a mainstay, providing the musical finale to each of the eight shows. 'We did those numbers on location. We were away filming and over dinner one night it started to snow. And all these dancers – 18-, 19-year-old girls – they'd never seen snow before. So they ran outside and started to play in it. We old seasoned campaigners stayed inside with a bottle of red wine.'

The shows were a huge success; if the Ronnies were more popular anywhere than they were in Britain, then it was Australia. 'I remember shaking hands with Ronnie at the end of the series and saying, "Well, that's it." He was very good about me retiring. He was terribly good. I could foresee him being upset or disturbed by it, but he was fine. And he's done very well for himself since. I'm so glad about that because we're still very good friends.'

'He told me 18 months in advance,' recalls Corbett. 'We were down along the coast

'He told me 18 months in advance. I was sort of surprised and **GOBSMACKED**... I wasn't absolutely shattered or mortally wounded in any way. **JUST SAD.**'

RONNIE CORBETT

Ronnie with old friend Josephine Tewson in his final sitcom, Clarence.

somewhere filming a Norseman sketch and we were having breakfast in the caravan and he said, "I have to tell you I've decided to retire. The Christmas show after the next one is the last show I'm going to do." I was sort of surprised and gobsmacked. But because he'd given me so much notice and we were so independent as well, I was just surprised and sad that he was going to have to do that and we would no longer do the show. But I wasn't absolutely shattered or mortally wounded in any way. Just sad. But I think he probably did it at the right time. It was getting difficult to find the gear and we'd have had to rethink. I knew he meant it. I doubt he would have said it to me without having really thought it through before. And I knew that he wasn't feeling very well, and that he was finding the strain of the writing, so it was a natural time to break off.'

Haven't I Seen You Somewhere Before, Clarence?

The two Ronnies stayed in Oz for four months this time, during which Ronnie B wrote his next and final sitcom, *Clarence*. It had been contracted, as had another *Ronnies* Christmas special, so he worked his time out, always aware that these would be his final professional engagements. *Clarence* began life as Fred, *The Removals Person* of Hugh Leonard's 1971 *Six Dates With Barker* episode. Like so many things in Ronnie's career, it was an idea that had stuck with him, something he returned to and developed. The first episode was a virtual remake of the original with both Josephine Tewson and Phyllida Law along for the ride one last time. Ronnie, of course, once again played the short-sighted removals man who teams up with Jo Tewson's maid, setting up home in the country, sharing a bed and slowly working their way towards marriage.

This time Ronnie wrote the show under the name Bob Ferris. It wasn't an intentional reference, yet one can't help but imagine that it was something of an unconscious homage to Clement and La Frenais, Bob Ferris being the name of Rodney Bewes' *Likely Lad*. 'I had arranged that I would not retire until the end of '87 and if you're not retired you want to be working. So I'd planned I go to Australia, come back and film *Clarence* in the spring of '87. Then I had a few weeks off and prepared for the *Two Ronnies* Christmas show. So it was fine. It was spaced out nicely. It wasn't a sudden thing. It was arranged.' There was, inevitably, a poignancy in writing and filming *Clarence*, knowing full well that it would the last time he did either.

There's a lovely circularity to Ronnie Barker's career. Peter Hall brought him to London and Peter Hall's offer led him to retire. He grew up in Oxford and for his final TV show he ensured that the location filming was done in Oxfordshire, a place he had begun to find his way back to ever since he bought his mill house back in 1981. 'I was coming back to my roots. Absolutely. So when I was writing *Clarence*, I thought, "I'll write this round the corner." I also wanted the country thing and the fact that this cockney man didn't know anything about the country. I enjoyed that sort of peasant thing. And he was very naïve. I'd enjoyed it when I'd done the original, I thought this character has potential.'

He may well have had potential, but the show's impact was inevitably leavened by the previous week's bombshell. When *Clarence* began its run in January 1988, the message may well have been inadvertent but it was nonetheless clear – don't get too attached to this man, he won't be coming back.

The Last Of The Ronnies

The recording of the final *Two Ronnies* Christmas special was going to be the last time Ronnie Barker ever set foot in a television studio. Among the show's guests was an unexpected slice of Hollywood glamour in the form of Charlton Heston. 'He'd never heard of us. We were allowed half an hour for shooting. His manager said, "We will arrive at 10.30 and we will leave at 11am." And poor old Mary Husband, who was our costume designer for most of the *Two Ronnies*, had failed to get part of his costume. His waistcoat hadn't arrived. And his manager arrived and said, "Mr Heston's waiting in the car. I just came to see if you're ready for him." And we said, "Unfortunately, we've got a bit of a problem with the costume." "What?!" – his manager really went mad. So I looked down at myself and I was wearing a waistcoat and I said, "What about this one?" So he came in and said, "Call me Chuck," straight away and Mary explained that the only waistcoat we've got is Mr Barker's. And he was fine. It was all hype from his manager.'

He almost changed it on the night. That famous line. Ronnie Barker was sitting there in front of his last studio audience, delivering his last news item and he almost changed it. 'And it's goodnight from him,' very nearly became 'And it's goodbye from me.' But it didn't. He knew people would notice. They'd ask too many questions. Ever the professional, Ronnie knew it would take away from the show. So he left quietly, after a drink with Ronnie C and their wives in a dressing room with the name 'Gerald Wiley' on the door. 'I remember we had this big Disney-like set for this piece we were doing, *Pinnochio II: Killer Doll*. I was at one end of it and I walked from one side to the other, through this

Ronnie B and Ronnie C as they will always be remembered; at a party.

'If you're not retired you want to be working.
So I'd planned I go to **AUSTRALIA**,
come back and film Clarence *in the spring of '87.*
Then I had a **FEW WEEKS OFF**
and prepared for the
Two Ronnies Christmas show'

glade and up over this little rustic bridge and I was thinking then this is the last time I was going to be on a set. I was very emotional. But all on my own. It was lovely. There was no one about. So I just lingered about a bit and said goodbye to it, really. And since then, nothing.'

It was a poignant evening for Ronnie Corbett as well: 'I remember it being a rather sad evening in a way because nobody knew, apart from Anne and I. I don't think he'd told anybody that it was going to be the last time he was in a BBC studio. I don't think he'd even told the technical crew. So we were all ending the show and saying our goodbyes and Anne and I and Joy and Ronnie went off and had a curry in Westbourne Grove. That was the last time he was going to do anything like that. So it was a bit sad and lonely, really, because he hadn't made a thing of it. It was touching, though, that it was only the four of us. In a way, for me it was quite moving that he'd done it so quietly.'

A Full Life

Fifty-eight. It's a funny age to retire. Especially for an actor. They just go on, don't they? Nobody really thought he meant it. Still, ten years on, people can't quite believe it, Ronnie Corbett included. But for Ronnie Barker there have been no regrets. He and Joy opened an antique shop in the nearby town of Chipping Norton called The Emporium. The locals know him and, ironically, in the wake of Arkwright, think of him now as a shopkeeper, even though Ronnie and Joy only work the shop themselves on the occasional Saturday. It's a sideline.

Public appearances since then have been few and far between. In 1996, he sat with Ronnie C, celebrating the BBC's anniversary and unexpectedly picked up a Lifetime Achievement in Comedy award. 'We were in the studio that we used to do *Two Ronnies* in. It was an audience full of famous faces. So it was wonderful when Michael Parkinson said at the end, "There's one

Ronnie and David Jason.

more award to come." I had no idea. He said, "This is an actor who retired eight years ago," and I thought, "Who else? I retired eight years ago." And Ronnie looked at me and said, "It must be you." It was a wonderfully proud moment, because they all stood up. I was so proud of that but I was obviously thinking on my feet because I thought, "No one's going to see them standing up," so I said, "Thank you very much ladies and gentlemen, please sit down." That was a career thing, really. Something in me said make sure that people know that your peers stood up. It was a strange feeling. In the middle of all this surprise, I managed to do that. And I met Robert Lindsay at the party afterwards and he said, "Congratulations. I know why you said that." And he was absolutely right.'

The following year, he appeared in the celebrity-packed audience of Ronnie C's TV special *An Audience With Ronnie Corbett*. 'I felt it was a bit of a lumber having him come along to the *Audience With...*' said Ronnie C, 'because he doesn't like those sorts of things. But it was very important for me to have him there. And it was a lovely last shot as the credits ran with him going, "More! more!" People loved to see him there, and they love to see me at his dos.' It meant a lot, of course, to have him there, but still there was something strange about seeing the two of them together... and yet not.

Rumours of his coming out of retirement were again sparked by a brief appearance at the 1997 Royal Command Performance. The *Two Ronnies*, appearing on television for the first time in a decade, rode on in disguise as TV chefs the *Two Fat Ladies*. Nobody knew about it and the ovation that greeted their appearance was a genuine outpouring from the audience, even though they were just there to introduce another act. 'I was asked to do something in it and they said Ronnie C was going to be doing something. And I said, "I'm retired, I'm not going to do

'*I don't think* **HE'D EVEN TOLD** *the technical crew. So we were all ending the show and saying our* **GOODBYES** *and Anne and I and Joy and Ronnie went off and had a* **CURRY** *in Westbourne Grove... It was touching, though, that it was only* **THE FOUR OF US**. *In a way for me it was quite moving that he'd done it so quietly*'

RONNIE CORBETT

anything." But I'd had this idea that we could look exactly like the *Two Fat Ladies* and I'd said to my wife some months earlier if Ronnie and I were still working together we'd definitely be doing them. Ronnie's bit eventually fell through and he was just left with introducing someone. So I explained the bit to him and he thought it was great. I rang up the director and said I will just introduce someone, providing I can get Ronnie to do it and I think I can. I'd already got him to do it, of course. And they thought the idea was marvellous. We kept it a secret and it went wonderfully well. And as we came off Jim Davidson was standing in the wings and he said, "Oh, thanks very much." '

Afterwards, Prince Phillip summed it up best

when he greeted Ronnie in the post-show line-up: 'Ah. They've exhumed you, have they?' But, sadly, they hadn't. Anyone hoping that the roar of the greasepaint and the smell of the crowd would lure Ronnie back were once again disappointed. 'All it stirred in me was the feeling of how proud and pleased I was, and am, that I'd made all those people laugh during my career, because I think it's better to make people laugh than cry. I would rather have been this actor who was funny than be a great Shakespearean actor who had moved people. That's what came back to me then. The length of the applause just went beyond the pleasure of seeing us. They suddenly realised, I think, that they were saying thank you for the whole thing. And that's when the

Ronnie and Joy Barker, enjoying their quiet life to the full.

applause took off and it carried on for a long time. But it didn't make me feel that I wanted to get back. It was just marvellous how much they appreciated it all. We were lucky enough to provide that laughter for so many years.'

The offers still come, of course, but they're not considered. People respect what Ronnie did but both within the industry and certainly among the public, they miss him. Millions of people welcomed Ronnie Barker into their homes on a weekly basis. Now he's not there there's a hole. Repeats are like looking at old photographs, they're a nice memory but they're not as good as the real thing. We have to get used to the fact that that's all we've got.

What remains is a comic legacy that endures and improves with age. Ronnie Barker did it all. Until there was nothing left to do, no ambitions left to fulfil.

Except one. 'Someone once said, "In life, you must have some ambition left," and I said my one ambition is to own a tree on which mistletoe is growing.'

Somewhere in the Cotswolds, outside a picturesque mill house, a small tree grows. And on that tree, some mistletoe blooms. That's a full life. ᗡᗡ

Career

FILMOGRAPHY

Wonderful Things! (1958)
Kill Or Cure (1962)
The Cracksman (1963)
Doctor In Distress (1963)
Father Came Too (1963)
The Bargee (1964)
A Home Of Your Own (1964)
Runaway Railway (1965)
The Man Outside (1967)
A Ghost Of A Chance (1967)
Futtock's End (1970)
The Magnificent Seven Deadly Sins (1971)
Robin And Marian (1976)
Porridge (1979)

TV-OGRAPHY

I'm Not Bothered (Series – 1959)
The Keys Of The Cafe (TV play)
The Holly Road Rig (TV play)
Six Faces Of Jim (1962)
Six More Faces Of Jim (Series – 6 episodes – co-star – 1962)
Tonight (in human comic strip – *Evelyn* – 1962)
More Faces Of Jim (Series – 6 episodes – co-star – 1963)
Sykes: Sykes And The Log Cabin (1964)
Charley's Aunt (TV play – 1965)
Before The Fringe (1965)
Not Only... But Also... (1965)
A Tale Of Two Cities (1965)
Gaslight Theatre (Series – 6 plays – 1965)

The Frost Report:
> Series regular
> 1st series – 13 episodes – 1966
> 2nd series – 13 episodes – 1967

plus **Frost Over Christmas** (special – 1967).
Foreign Affairs (series, 6 episodes, 1966)
The Saint: The Better Mousetrap (1966)
Crackerjack (1967)
The Avengers: The Hidden Tiger (1967)
The Ronnie Barker Playhouse (1968)
> Tennyson
> Ah, There You Are
> The Fastest Gun In Finchley
> The Incredible Mr Tanner
> Talk Of Angels
> Alexander

Frost On Sunday: Series regular
> 1st series – 23 episodes – 1969
> 2nd series – 12 episodes – 1970

Hark At Barker
> 1st series – 8 episodes -1969
> 2nd series – 7 episodes -1970

Six Dates With Barker (1971)
> 1937: The Removals Person
> 1899: The Phantom Raspberry Blower Of Old London Town
> 1970: The Odd Job
> 1915: Lola
> 1971: Come In And Lie Down
> 2774: All the World's A Stooge

The Ronnie Barker Yearbook (1971)
Ronnie Corbett In Bed (1971)
The Two Ronnies (12 series – 94 episodes – 1971-1986)
A Midsummer Night's Dream (TV play – 1972)
His Lordship Entertains (series – 7 episodes – 1972)
Comedy Playhouse: Idle At Work (1972)
Seven Of One (1973)
> Open All Hours
> Prisoner And Escort
> My Old Man
> Spanner's Eleven
> Another Fine Mess
> One Man's Meat
> I'll Fly You For A Quid

Porridge (1974 – 1977)
> (3 series – 18 episodes including Prisoner And Escort pilot;
> plus 2 Christmas specials 1975, 1976)

When We Are Married (TV Play – 1975)
The Picnic (1976)
Open All Hours (1976. 1981 – 1985)
         (4 series – 25 episodes)
The Best Of The Two Ronnies (TV special – 1977)
By The Sea (TV special – 1982)
The Magnificent Evans (Series – 6 episodes – 1984)
The Two Ronnies (Australia) (Series – 7 episodes – 1986)
20 Years Of The Two Ronnies (Series – 8 episodes – 1986)
21 Years Of The Two Ronnies (Series – 8 episodes – 1987)
Clarence (Series – 6 episodes – 1988)
22 Years Of The Two Ronnies (Series – 8 episodes -1988)
An Audience With Ronnie Corbett (TV special – 1996)
The Royal Variety Performance (TV special – 1997)

RADIOGRAPHY

The Floggits (BBC 1958)
The Navy Lark (BBC – 1959 – 1968)
Variety Playhouse (BBC 1961-1963)
Round The Bend (1961)
Crowther's Crowd (BBC – 1963)
Not To Worry (BBC – 1964)
Let's Face It (BBC – 1965)
Lines from My Grandfather's Forehead (BBC – 2 series of 8 episodes, plus **Lines From My Grandfather's Christmas Forehead Special** – 1971-1972)

DISCOGRAPHY

Irma La Douce (LP cast recording – 1958)
On The Brighter Side (LP cast recording 1961)
The Frost Report On Everything (LP TV compilation 1968)
A Pint Of Old And Filthy (LP 1969)
Vintage Variety (LP compilation includes *Crowther's Crowd* extract – 1973)
Fifty Years of Radio Comedy (LP compilation with *Navy Lark* extract – 1973)
Jehosaphat And Jones (LP 1973)
The Best Of The Two Ronnies (LP 1976)
The Two Ronnies (LP 1976)
Comedy Spectacular (LP compilation with *Two Ronnies* extract 1976)
The Two Ronnies – Vol 2 (1977)
Porridge (LP 1977)
Comedy Special (LP compilation with *Porridge* and *Two Ronnies* extracts – 1977)
The Two Ronnies – Vol 3 (1978)
Ronnie Barker's Unbroken British Record (LP 1978)
Going Straight/String Bean Queen (single 1978)
Fun At One (LP compilation with *Two Ronnies* extract – 1979)
The Two Ronnies – Vol 4 (1980)
More Fun At One (LP includes *Two Ronnies* extract – 1980)
The Laughing Stock Of The BBC (LP includes *Two Ronnies* extracts – 1982)
We Are Most Amused (LP includes *Two Ronnies* extract – 1982)
The Very Best Of Me And The Very Best Of Him (LP 1984)

BOOKS BY RONNIE BARKER:

Ronnie Barker's Book Of Bathing Beauties (1974)
Ronnie Barker's Book Of Boudoir Beauties (1975)
It's Goodnight From Him (1976)
Sauce (1977)
Gentleman's Relish (1979)
Fletcher's Book Of Rhyming Slang (1979)
Sugar And Spice (1981)
Ooh-la-la! The Ladies Of Paris (1983)
Pebbles On The Beach (1985)
A Pennyworth Of Art (1986)
It's Hello – From Him (1988)
Dancing In The Moonlight (1993)

RONNIE BARKER AWARDS

Variety Club Entertainer Of The Year – 1969, 1974, 1980
Society Of Film And Television Arts – 1971
Radio Industries Club – 1973, 1974, 1977, 1981
Water Rats Entertainer Of The Year – 1975
BAFTA: Television Comedy Actor Of The Year – 1975, 1977, 1978
Royal Television Society's Award For Outstanding Creative Achievement – 1975
British Comedy Award For Lifetime Achievement – 1990
BBC Lifetime Achievement In Comedy Award – 1996

SOURCES

Dancing in The Moonlight by Ronnie Barker (Coronet 1994)
Radio Comedy 1938 – 1968 by Andy Foster and Steve Furst (Virgin 1996)
The Reluctant Jester by Michael Bentine (Transworld 1992)
Just Keep Talking by Steve Wright with Peter Compton (Simon & Schuster, 1997)
The Guinness Book Of Classic British TV by Paul Cornell, Martin Day and Keith Topping (Guinness 1996)
Laugh Magazine
The Radio Times
The Daily Mail
The Guardian
The Daily Mirror
The Times
The Daily Express
The Daily Telegraph
The Daily Star
Today
Evening News
Evening Standard
(... **Not the Sun**!)

PHOTOGRAPHS

Except as listed below all pictures are courtesy of Mr. Ronnie Barker, from his personal collection

ABC – page 51, **ALPHA** - pages 17, 97, 101, 108, Dave Bennett/ALPHA – 11, 129, 130,
A Davidson/ALPHA - 137, **BBC** – pages 72, 75, 95, 103, 111 115, 119, 121, 124, 128, 131, 138, 140,
KEN HAWARD, courtesy of Mr. Ronnie Barker – pages 33, 47, **PICTORIAL** – page 135,
SCOPE – pages 76, 91, 92, 100, 107, 117, **UPP** – Cover, page 84.